AMERICAN POETS PROJECT

AMERICAN POETS PROJECT

IS PUBLISHED WITH A GIFT IN MEMORY OF

James Merrill

AND SUPPORT FROM ITS FOUNDING PATRONS

Sidney J. Weinberg, Jr. Foundation

The Berkley Foundation

Richard B. Fisher and Jeanne Donovan Fisher

Theodore Roethke

selected poems

edward hirsch editor

AMERICAN POETS PROJECT

THE LIBRARY OF AMERICA

The paper used in this publication meets the requirements of ANSI/NISO Z39.48–1992 (Permanence of Paper).

Frontispiece: Theodore Roethke, 1952, photo by James O. Sneddon. University of Washington Libraries, Special Collections, UW 20147Z.

Library of Congress Control Number: 2024942663
ISBN: 978–1–59853–795–6

First paperback printing – November 2024

10 9 8 7 6 5 4 3 2 1

Theodore
Roethke

CONTENTS

INTRODUCTION   xiii

from *Open House* (1941)

   Open House   1
   The Premonition   2
   Mid-Country Blow   2
   The Heron   3
   The Bat   3
   "Long Live the Weeds"   4
   On the Road to Woodlawn   4
   Highway: Michigan   5
   Night Journey   6

from *The Lost Son and Other Poems* (1948)

   Cuttings   7
   Cuttings: later   7
   Root Cellar   8
   Forcing House   8
   Weed Puller   9
   Orchids   10
   Moss-Gathering   10
   Big Wind   11

Old Florist   12

Frau Bauman, Frau Schmidt, and Frau Schwartze   13

Transplanting   14

Child on Top of a Greenhouse   15

Flower Dump   16

Carnations   16

My Papa's Waltz   17

Pickle Belt   17

Dolor   18

Double Feature   19

The Return   19

Night Crow   20

River Incident   20

The Minimal   21

The Waking   21

The Lost Son   23

The Long Alley   30

A Field of Light   34

The Shape of the Fire   36

from *Praise to the End!* (1951)

Where Knock Is Open Wide   41

I Need, I Need   45

Praise to the End!   48

Unfold! Unfold!   52

I Cry, Love! Love!   55

from *The Waking* (1953)

O, Thou Opening, O   58

A Light Breather   62

Elegy for Jane   63

from Four for Sir John Davies: The Dance   64

The Waking   65

from *Words for the Wind* (1958)

Words for the Wind   66

I Knew a Woman   70

The Sententious Man 71
The Pure Fury 73
The Surly One 74
The Beast 75
A Walk in Late Summer 76
Snake 77
Slug 78
from Meditations of an Old Woman: First Meditation 79

from *The Far Field* (1964)

North American Sequence
  The Longing 84
  Meditation at Oyster River 86
  Journey to the Interior 90
  The Long Waters 94
  The Far Field 97
  The Rose 102
Elegy 107
Otto 108
The Meadow Mouse 110
Heard in a Violent Ward 111
The Geranium 111
The Storm 113
The Thing 115
from Sequence, Sometimes Metaphysical
  In a Dark Time 116
  The Sequel 117
  The Right Thing 118

POEMS FOR CHILDREN

Dinky 120
The Cow 121
The Serpent 121
The Sloth 122
The Lady and the Bear 123
The Kitty-Cat Bird 124

The Whale   125

The Yak   125

The Donkey   125

The Hippo   126

The Lamb   126

The Lizard   126

FROM THE NOTEBOOKS   127

Biographical Note   147

Note on the Texts   149

Notes   151

Index of Titles and First Lines 154

INTRODUCTION

I proclaim once more a condition of joy.
                    —THEODORE ROETHKE

Theodore Roethke pitted himself against oblivion—"I practice at walking the void," he said—and was not afraid of the strange, the uncanny, the mysterious. He courted the irrational and embraced what is most vulnerable in life. "Those who are willing to be vulnerable move among mysteries," he declared. I love the way he celebrated and moralized the American landscape, schooled his spirit in the marsh and mire, and transformed himself into a major romantic poet. Readers of this new *Selected Poems* will find a worthy successor to Whitman and Emerson, our quintessential philosopher who proposed that "there are two absorbing facts: *I and the Abyss.*" Here is a mid-twentieth-century American poet who self-consciously inherited and extended the romantic tradition of Yeats, Stevens, and Crane, and belongs to that visionary company.

Roethke grew up in the harsh soil and savage climate of Michigan, where his German-American family owned a 25-acre greenhouse, one of the largest in the Midwest, in the Saginaw Valley. (It was gossiped that the Roethkes had "Ein Nagel im Kopf"—a nail in the head, a vernacular expression that suggests arrogant eccentricity.) The countryside was flat and vast, and he often wandered the far fields. He dwelled in the midst of rocks and plants, weeds and moss, flowers of all kinds (his father specialized in orchids and roses). Subsequently, the "tropical" world of the greenhouse came to stand for the lost world of his childhood and, at the same time, to serve as the central symbol —both the heaven and hell—of his poetry.

Roethke was a young teenager when his father died (Otto Roethke was an indomitable man with a strong Prussian temperament and a delicate gift for growing things) and the kingdom of his childhood collapsed. As his biographer Allan Seager points out, "what he lost when the dirt fell in his father's grave was going to take him the rest of his life to learn." Nothing more momentous ever happened to him, and his Oedipal love and fear of his father ("My Papa's Waltz" captures the furious duality of his feeling) was inextricably intertwined with his complex, idiosyncratic feelings for nature. As he recalled in the poem "Otto," which he wrote near the end his life:

In my mind's eye I see those fields of glass,
As I looked at them from the high house,
Riding beneath the moon, hid from the moon,
Then slowly breaking whiter in the dawn;
When George the watchman's lantern dropped from sight
The long pipes knocked: it was the end of night.
I'd stand upon my bed, a sleepless child
Watching the waking of my father's world.—
O world so far away! O my lost world!

Roethke never entirely recovered from his childhood, but like a gritty, roaring, postwar American version of Rilke, he turned it into a fertile source for art. It was the feeling for his vanished Midwestern childhood as well as his sense of forever being "the lost son"—to use the title of his second book—that first drew me to his poetry.

The deep-seated struggle and determination to become a poet is one of the defining features of Roethke's life. He possessed what in a student essay he called "a driving sincerity," and all his life regarded himself as an initiate, a "perpetual beginner." He loved the catchy, strongly stressed rhythms of children's verse, of Mother Goose and other folk material, and incorporated them into hilarious nonsense poems and innovative long sequences. A childlike orality ("I sing a small sing") with an undertow of need or longing is one of the distinguishing marks of his poetry.

> Snail, snail, glister me forward,
> Bird, soft-sigh me home,
> Worm, be with me.
> This is my hard time.

Roethke caressed the primitive sounds of words and believed that "repetition in word and phrase and in idea is the very essence of poetry." Repetition suited his obsessions. He was devoted to poetry as a form of "memorable speech" and struggled to compete with his own supreme masters. There was something abject and beautiful about the way that he devoured other poets whole (from John Donne and Sir John Davies to Emily Dickinson, W. H. Auden and Léonie Adams) and survived his own overwhelming influences. In this way, he was a sort of Arshile Gorky of modern American poetry. "The Kitty-Cat Bird" takes this subject of influence into the parabolic realm of nonsense poetry ("Be sure that whatever you are is you").

A revealing prose piece is called "How to Write Like Somebody Else."

One thinks of him as a huge dancing-bear of a man, a heavy drinker, a "ring-tailed roarer." He had gargantuan emotional needs, disabling insecurities, and insatiable appetites. He sought out mentors and made strong early friendships with Rolfe Humphries and Louise Bogan, with whom he had a tumultuous love affair that metamorphosed into a sweet, lifelong attachment. (His essay "The Poetry of Louise Bogan" is still the best short piece ever written about her work.) He showed up unannounced at Stanley Kunitz's house in the Delaware Valley, mumbling compliments and clutching a copy of Kunitz's first book tucked under his left paw. They stayed up all night drinking and talking about poetry. "The image that never left me," Kunitz later remembered, "was of a blond, smooth, shambling giant, irrevocably Teutonic, with a cold pudding of a face, somehow contradicted by the sullen downturn of the mouth and the pale furious eyes: a countenance ready to be touched by time, waiting to be transfigured, with a few subtle lines, into a tragic mask."

Roethke had what he wryly called "a full-life complex." He was unabashedly sensual—at times shy and gentle, at times verbose and aggressive. He had an antic, ribald sense of humor and was outsize in everything he did. He overcompensated for his extreme sensitivity with a masculine notion that "poets are tough." He railed against the literary establishment, "the tweed-coated cliché masters." He was a competitive tennis player, surprisingly agile on his feet, with a titanic serve and a thunderous forehand. He started out teaching English to undergraduates, took his duties as a college tennis coach seriously ("Roethke, Penn State Tennis Coach, Author of Book of Verses," the New York *Herald Tribune* announced in its "Sports Here and

There" column in March 1941), and could never stand to lose at anything.

Over the years Roethke became a famously gifted teacher, who invested a tremendous amount of energy in teaching poetry (he once said it was like "lugging . . . hunks of pork up the lower slopes of Parnassus") and worked with great intensity on his own lyrics. He did significant stints at Lafayette College, Pennsylvania State University, Bennington College, and the University of Washington, where he taught for the last fifteen years of his life. He taught his students to revel in the sounds of words, which flooded him with pleasure, and communicated his passion for verse forms of all sorts. He praised verbal immediacy and paid special attention to texture, rhythm, energy ("Energy is the soul of poetry"), the unit of breath, the specific emotion. "Poetry-writing (the craft) can't be taught," he noted, "but it can be insinuated." He also said, "I am overwhelmed by the beautiful disorder of poetry, the eternal virginity of words." Some of his key early pupils at the University of Washington were Carolyn Kizer, James Wright, and David Wagoner. Among other things, his notebooks demonstrate his passion for teaching ("One teaches out of love") and testify to how hard he concentrated on making and assembling poems, how seriously he took his own vocation. He fought for recognition and near the end of his life sarcastically referred to himself as "the oldest younger poet in the U.S.A."

Roethke's life was characterized by a series of highs and lows, a recurring cycle of manic episodes and severe mental breakdowns. He was periodically hospitalized and occasionally given shock treatments. His suffering was dramatic and intense. An extremist of the imagination, he purposefully seemed to disorder his senses. (He married Beatrice O'Connell late in life and told his young wife that his first psychotic episode had been self-induced "to reach a new level of reality.") He was forthright about his manic-depression ("What's madness," he wrote, "but nobility of soul / At odds with circumstance?") and identified strongly with other joyous and mystical poets of romantic madness. "In heaven, too, / You'd be institutionalized. / But that's all right," he declared in "Heard in a Violent Ward." "If they let you eat and swear / With the likes of Blake, / and Christopher Smart, / And that sweet man, John Clare."

Roethke's first book, *Open House* (1941), took him ten years to write. It is notable for its compact lyricism, its technical resourcefulness, and its witty, neo-metaphysical manner. The hard-working and highly susceptible young poet took his lead from T. S. Eliot's central essay on metaphysical poetry, and was influenced, perhaps too heavily, by John Donne, George Herbert, and Henry Vaughan. He also showed what would turn out to be a characteristically keen eye for marshes and waste places ("Long live the weeds"), for herons and bats. My own favorite poem in the collection, "Night Journey," captures the feeling of a train ride back to Michigan, the heart of the country, and suggests something of his natural sensitivity to American landscapes.

Roethke himself later criticized the "chilly fastidiousness" and austere vision of his apprentice collection. Undoubtedly, the greatest single moment in his writing life was the breakthrough from the abstract strictures of his early manner into the textured free verse of his second collection, *The Lost Son and Other Poems* (1948). His first book made a confessional promise—"my secrets cry aloud" and "my heart keeps open house"—that his second book fulfilled. He found his core poetic when he made contact with the loamy soil of his Michigan childhood ("I can hear, underground, that sucking and sobbing, / In my veins, in my bones I feel it"). The figure of the open house gives way to the discovery, the memory, of the glass enclosure, a hothouse world that he once called "a symbol for the whole of life, a womb, a heaven-on-earth."

The family greenhouse was for Roethke both sacred and abysmal ground, simultaneously a natural world and an artificial realm, a locale of generation and decay, order and chaos. It was wilderness brought home. The fourteen "greenhouse poems" explore the instinctual sources of life from the dank minimal world of roots in "Root Cellar" ("What a congress of stinks!") to the open, flowering reality of young plants in "Transplanting" ("The whole flower extending outward, / Stretching and reaching"). He plunged into the dirt and returned to the sunlit realms of "Child on Top of a Greenhouse," where the daredevil boy is an embryonic artist. What compelled him was "news of the root," the vigorous green force of plant life.

> This urge, wrestle, resurrection of dry sticks,
> Cut stems struggling to put down feet,
> What saint strained so much,
> Rose on such lopped limbs to a new life?

Roethke was compulsively conscious of the agony of birth, the painful effort of things to emerge out of an underworld swarming with malevolent forces. There is a sense of "tugging all day at perverse life" in "Weed Puller" ("Me down in that fetor of weeds, / Crawling on all fours, / Alive in a slippery grave"), of plants that are like strange reptiles in "Orchids" ("So many devouring infants!"), of tearing the ground and disturbing the natural rhythms of the living planet in "Moss Gathering," of ferocious adult sexuality in "Big Wind," of one surviving tulip swaggering "over the dying, the newly dead" in "Flower Dump." These poems go underground to dark obsessive realms and then chart the struggle back up for light.

The greenhouse was also linked to two other discoveries Roethke made in the 1940s. Largely prompted by his friend Kenneth Burke, who later wrote an insightful essay on his "vegetal radicalism," Roethke began to explore the poetic possibilities of the unconscious, returning to the realms of childhood and thus commencing "the retrospective course" of his "hallucinatory dream." He also recognized that the organic process of plants could stand as a metaphor for free verse, each poem taking on its own sensuous form and intrinsic shape. This was an Emersonian notion of poetic form, a fundamental of romantic expressiveness, and it enabled Roethke to become the figure that John Berryman dubbed "The Garden Master."

Roethke's central sequence of dramatic interior monologues begins with the title poem of *The Lost Son*, continues with *Praise to the End!* (1951), which takes its name from Wordsworth, and concludes with the opening lyric of *The Waking* (1953). These poems are a kind of spiritual autobiography. "Each poem is complete in itself," he wrote, "yet each . . . is a stage in a . . . struggle out of the slime; part of a slow spiritual progress; an effort to be born, and later, to become something more." This is an American poet's eccentric *Prelude*.

In a revealing "Open Letter," Roethke asserted:

Some of these pieces, then, begin in the mire; as if man is no more than a shape writhing from the old rock. This may be due, in part, to the Michigan from which I come. Sometimes one gets the feeling that not even the animals have been there before; but the marsh, the mire, the Void, is always there, immediate and terrifying. It is a splendid space for schooling the spirit. It is America.

Roethke was an American poet of the regressive imagination. He looked for guidance to the work of other modern poets who evoked the archaic to give their poems ritual power, such as W. B. Yeats, Robert Graves, D. H. Lawrence ("For Lawrence and I are going the same way: down: / a loosening in the dark"), and Dylan Thomas ("This rare heedless fornicator of language speaks with the voice of angels and ravens, casting us back where the sea leaps and the strudding witch walks by a deep well") .

In this way, Roethke was a key link in the chain to such startlingly regressive poets as Ted Hughes and Sylvia Plath, both of whom avowed his influence. He anticipated the deep image poetics—the pastoral ecstasy—of Robert Bly and James Wright, and heavily influenced the mythic parables of W. S. Merwin, Charles Simic, and Mark Strand. His goal was to recover the first primordial world of the psyche, indeed to write, as he formulated it, "a poem in the shape of the psyche under great stress." There was something primal, agitated, and earthy in his quest ("I want the old rage, the lash of primordial milk!"). He sought what ultimately may be unattainable: a direct presentation of the unconscious making itself known. His subject was birth and metamorphosis, the snake shedding its skin, the man struggling to regain, in Yeats's phrase, "radical innocence."

Roethke put language under intense pressure and developed a strange, highly kinetic, radically associative method—a sort of projective verse of the unconscious—to chart the struggle to be born, the progress "from I to Otherwise." He radically fragmented narratives, experimented with collage, and extended the possibilities of free verse. He extolled the irrational ("Reason? That dreary shed, that hutch for grubby schoolboys"), relied heavily on fairy tales and myths, riffed off nursery rhymes and Elizabethan songs, built on Blakean precedents, and mimicked biblical rhythms. His psychological task was to go backward in order to go forward, which is why first Freud and then Jung were such enabling presences for him. "I've crawled from the mire, alert as a saint or a dog," he declared, and, "I was far back, farther than anybody else."

There is a dimension of nonsense poetry as well as an element of shamanism in all this, as when the speaker suddenly calls out:

> Voice, come out of the silence.
> Say something.
> Appear in the form of a spider
> Or a moth beating the curtain.

And the voice comes back to him:

> Dark hollows said, lee to the wind,
> The moon said, back of an eel,
> The salt said, look by the sea,
> Your tears are not enough praise,
> You will find no comfort here,
> In the kingdom of bang and blab.

Grief is not praise and, strikingly, the sea refuses to comfort the human protagonist. And yet Roethke's psychological regression, like John Keats's negative capability, instills the natural world with soul. The poet would be a vehicle for the oracular language of nature. Roethke's special gift was palpable whenever he welcomed visceral spirits into his work ("The Depth calls to the Height"), or proclaimed a condition of pure joy, or channeled his madness by struggling "to catch the movement of the mind itself."

Roethke moved with unusual fluency between metrical and free verse, and he returned to traditional forms with great enthusiasm in *The Waking* (1953) and *Words for the Wind* (1958). He was at times overwhelmed by Yeats's power—he called it "daring to compete with papa" ("I take this cadence from a man named Yeats; / I take, and I give it back again")—but mostly fused the Irish master with the Elizabethan plain stylists to create a unique, end-stopped musical style. In his sensuous love poems, he uses poetry for the direct, as opposed to the abstract, apprehension of things. In "Words for the Wind" ("I bear, but not alone / The burden of this joy"), one of his own favorite poems, and "I Knew a Woman," he celebrated his young wife, the beloved, and expressed terrific joy at going beyond the self and living in the dynamic presence and light of another. Love becomes a way of triumphing over nonbeing and nothingness ("I measure time by how a body sways"), of transcending isolation and mystically uniting body and spirit.

Roethke loved to be carried away and transported by passion. Dance is thus one of the reigning metaphors of his work.

> Is that dance slowing in the mind of man
> That made him think the universe could hum?
> The great wheel turns its axle when it can;
> I need a place to sing, and dancing-room,
> And I have made a promise to my ears
> I'll sing and whistle romping with the bears.

He was happiest as a comic rhapsodist, as a metaphysical poet of "pure being," as James Dickey put it, who thought with his body. "There is no poetry anywhere," Dickey insisted, "that is so valuably conscious of the human body as Roethke's; no poetry that can place the body in an *environment*—wind, seascape, greenhouse, forest, desert, mountainside, among animals, or insects, or stones." "We think by feeling," Roethke declared in his villanelle "The Waking." "What is there to know?" He could feel his very being "dance from ear to ear."

The Far Field, published posthumously in 1964, has the feeling—the deep finality—of a last book. It has a couple of shocking poems about predators and victims, such as "The Thing" and "The Meadow Mouse," in which he identifies with "all things innocent, helpless, forsaken." I especially love the "North American Sequence," a group of six poems that have a deep meditative openness and fresh discursive energy. They have spiritual resolution.

Here Roethke consciously responds to Eliot's *Four Quartets*. He quotes "East Coker"—"Old men should be explorers?"—and offers an idea of the American poet as a wise primitive. "I'll be an Indian. / Ogalala? / Iroquois." Whereas Eliot moves eastward from the Midwest to New England and back to England itself, Roethke purposefully reverses direction and heads westward, driving from Michigan to the Dakotas to the Rockies to the Pacific Northwest. He puts himself under Whitman's shadow, his presiding spirit, and presents a passionate free-verse catalogue of the American continent. He ponders "how to transcend this sensual emptiness," even as he refuses to desert the natural world for a higher plane. "Beautiful is my desire," he asserts, "and the place of my desire." He becomes a writer of place ("There are those to whom place is unimportant, / But this place, where sea and fresh water meet, / Is important") and establishes himself as a poet of the egotistical sublime.

There are many stalled moments in the journey westward, a natural allegory, but there are also moments of radiant plenitude and visionary affirmation:

> As a blind man, lifting a curtain, knows it is morning,
> I know this change:
> On one side of silence there is no smile;
> But when I breathe with the birds,

> The spirit of wrath becomes the spirit of blessing,
> And the dead begin from their dark to sing in my
> sleep.

At such moments one feels the emotional truth of Roethke's claim that "in spite of all the muck and welter, the dark, the *dreck*, of these poems, I count myself among the happy poets." In the end, after so much suffering, Roethke embraced a spirit of blessing and achieved a final transformation, a consoling self-acceptance, solace of being, "the true ease of myself." He trusted joy. "I learned not to fear infinity, / The far field, the windy cliffs of forever," he declared. "And I rejoiced in being what I was."

Edward Hirsch
2004

Open House

My secrets cry aloud.
I have no need for tongue.
My heart keeps open house,
My doors are widely swung.
An epic of the eyes
My love, with no disguise.

My truths are all foreknown,
This anguish self-revealed.
I'm naked to the bone,
With nakedness my shield.
Myself is what I wear:
I keep the spirit spare.

The anger will endure,
The deed will speak the truth
In language strict and pure.
I stop the lying mouth:
Rage warps my clearest cry
To witless agony.

The Premonition

Walking this field I remember
Days of another summer.
Oh that was long ago! I kept
Close to the heels of my father,
Matching his stride with half-steps
Until we came to a river.
He dipped his hand in the shallow:
Water ran over and under
Hair on a narrow wrist bone;
His image kept following after,—
Flashed with the sun in the ripple.
But when he stood up, that face
Was lost in a maze of water.

Mid-Country Blow

All night and all day the wind roared in the trees,
Until I could think there were waves rolling high as my
        bedroom floor;
When I stood at the window, an elm bough swept to my
        knees;
The blue spruce lashed like a surf at the door.

The second dawn I would not have believed:
The oak stood with each leaf stiff as a bell.
When I looked at the altered scene, my eye was
        undeceived,
But my ear still kept the sound of the sea like a shell.

The Heron

The heron stands in water where the swamp
Has deepened to the blackness of a pool,
Or balances with one leg on a hump
Of marsh grass heaped above a musk-rat hole.

He walks the shallow with an antic grace.
The great feet break the ridges of the sand,
The long eye notes the minnow's hiding place.
His beak is quicker than a human hand.

He jerks a frog across his bony lip,
Then points his heavy bill above the wood.
The wide wings flap but once to lift him up.
A single ripple starts from where he stood.

The Bat

By day the bat is cousin to the mouse.
He likes the attic of an aging house.

His fingers make a hat about his head.
His pulse beat is so slow we think him dead.

He loops in crazy figures half the night
Among the trees that face the corner light.

But when he brushes up against a screen,
We are afraid of what our eyes have seen:

For something is amiss or out of place
When mice with wings can wear a human face.

"Long Live the Weeds"

—Hopkins

Long live the weeds that overwhelm
My narrow vegetable realm!
The bitter rock, the barren soil
That force the son of man to toil;
All things unholy, marred by curse,
The ugly of the universe.
The rough, the wicked, and the wild
That keep the spirit undefiled.
With these I match my little wit
And earn the right to stand or sit,
Hope, love, create, or drink and die:
These shape the creature that is I.

On the Road to Woodlawn

I miss the polished brass, the powerful black horses,
The drivers creaking the seats of the baroque hearses,
The high-piled floral offerings with sentimental verses,
The carriages reeking with varnish and stale perfume.

I miss the pallbearers momentously taking their places,
The undertaker's obsequious grimaces,
The craned necks, the mourners' anonymous faces,
—And the eyes, still vivid, looking up from a sunken
    room.

Highway: Michigan

Here from the field's edge we survey
The progress of the jaded. Mile
On mile of traffic from the town
Rides by, for at the end of day
The time of workers is their own.

They jockey for position on
The strip reserved for passing only.
The drivers from production lines
Hold to advantage dearly won.
They toy with death and traffic fines.

Acceleration is their need:
A mania keeps them on the move
Until the toughest nerves are frayed.
They are the prisoners of speed
Who flee in what their hands have made.

The pavement smokes when two cars meet
And steel rips through conflicting steel.
We shiver at the siren's blast.
One driver, pinned beneath the seat,
Escapes from the machine at last.

Night Journey

Now as the train bears west,
Its rhythm rocks the earth,
And from my Pullman berth
I stare into the night
While others take their rest.
Bridges of iron lace,
A suddenness of trees,
A lap of mountain mist
All cross my line of sight,
Then a bleak wasted place,
And a lake below my knees.
Full on my neck I feel
The straining at a curve;
My muscles move with steel,
I wake in every nerve.
I watch a beacon swing
From dark to blazing bright;
We thunder through ravines
And gullies washed with light.
Beyond the mountain pass
Mist deepens on the pane;
We rush into a rain
That rattles double glass.
Wheels shake the roadbed stone,
The pistons jerk and shove,
I stay up half the night
To see the land I love.

Cuttings

Sticks-in-a-drowse droop over sugary loam,
Their intricate stem-fur dries;
But still the delicate slips keep coaxing up water;
The small cells bulge;

One nub of growth
Nudges a sand-crumb loose,
Pokes through a musty sheath
Its pale tendrilous horn.

Cuttings

later

This urge, wrestle, resurrection of dry sticks,
Cut stems struggling to put down feet,
What saint strained so much,
Rose on such lopped limbs to a new life?

I can hear, underground, that sucking and sobbing,
In my veins, in my bones I feel it,—
The small waters seeping upward,
The tight grains parting at last.

When sprouts break out,
Slippery as fish,
I quail, lean to beginnings, sheath-wet.

Root Cellar

Nothing would sleep in that cellar, dank as a ditch,
Bulbs broke out of boxes hunting for chinks in the dark,
Shoots dangled and drooped,
Lolling obscenely from mildewed crates,
Hung down long yellow evil necks, like tropical snakes.
And what a congress of stinks!—
Roots ripe as old bait,
Pulpy stems, rank, silo-rich,
Leaf-mold, manure, lime, piled against slippery planks.
Nothing would give up life:
Even the dirt kept breathing a small breath.

Forcing House

Vines tougher than wrists
And rubbery shoots,
Scums, mildews, smuts along stems,
Great cannas or delicate cyclamen tips,—
All pulse with the knocking pipes
That drip and sweat,
Sweat and drip,

Swelling the roots with steam and stench,
Shooting up lime and dung and ground bones,—
Fifty summers in motion at once,
As the live heat billows from pipes and pots.

Weed Puller

Under the concrete benches,
Hacking at black hairy roots,—
Those lewd monkey-tails hanging from drainholes,—
Digging into the soft rubble underneath,
Webs and weeds,
Grubs and snails and sharp sticks,
Or yanking tough fern-shapes,
Coiled green and thick, like dripping smilax,
Tugging all day at perverse life:
The indignity of it!—
With everything blooming above me,
Lilies, pale-pink cyclamen, roses,
Whole fields lovely and inviolate,—
Me down in that fetor of weeds,
Crawling on all fours,
Alive, in a slippery grave.

Orchids

They lean over the path,
Adder-mouthed,
Swaying close to the face,
Coming out, soft and deceptive,
Limp and damp, delicate as a young bird's tongue;
Their fluttery fledgling lips
Move slowly,
Drawing in the warm air.

And at night,
The faint moon falling through whitewashed glass,
The heat going down
So their musky smell comes even stronger,
Drifting down from their mossy cradles:
So many devouring infants!
Soft luminescent fingers,
Lips neither dead nor alive,
Loose ghostly mouths
Breathing.

Moss-Gathering

To loosen with all ten fingers held wide and limber
And lift up a patch, dark-green, the kind for lining
          cemetery baskets,
Thick and cushiony, like an old-fashioned doormat,
The crumbling small hollow sticks on the underside
          mixed with roots,

And wintergreen berries and leaves still stuck to the
      top,—
That was moss-gathering.
But something always went out of me when I dug loose
      those carpets
Of green, or plunged to my elbows in the spongy
      yellowish moss of the marshes:
And afterwards I always felt mean, jogging back over the
      logging road,
As if I had broken the natural order of things in that
      swampland;
Disturbed some rhythm, old and of vast importance,
By pulling off flesh from the living planet;
As if I had committed, against the whole scheme of life,
      a desecration.

Big Wind

Where were the greenhouses going,
Lunging into the lashing
Wind driving water
So far down the river
All the faucets stopped?—
So we drained the manure-machine
For the steam plant,
Pumping the stale mixture
Into the rusty boilers,
Watching the pressure gauge
Waver over to red,

As the seams hissed
And the live steam
Drove to the far
End of the rose-house,
Where the worst wind was,
Creaking the cypress window-frames,
Cracking so much thin glass
We stayed all night,
Stuffing the holes with burlap;
But she rode it out,
That old rose-house,
She hove into the teeth of it,
The core and pith of that ugly storm,
Ploughing with her stiff prow,
Bucking into the wind-waves
That broke over the whole of her,
Flailing her sides with spray,
Flinging long strings of wet across the roof-top,
Finally veering, wearing themselves out, merely
Whistling thinly under the wind-vents;
She sailed until the calm morning,
Carrying her full cargo of roses.

Old Florist

That hump of a man bunching chrysanthemums
Or pinching-back asters, or planting azaleas,
Tamping and stamping dirt into pots,—
How he could flick and pick

Rotten leaves or yellowy petals,
Or scoop out a weed close to flourishing roots,
Or make the dust buzz with a light spray,
Or drown a bug in one spit of tobacco juice,
Or fan life into wilted sweet-peas with his hat,
Or stand all night watering roses, his feet blue in rubber
    boots.

Frau Bauman, Frau Schmidt, and Frau Schwartze

Gone the three ancient ladies
Who creaked on the greenhouse ladders,
Reaching up white strings
To wind, to wind
The sweet-pea tendrils, the smilax,
Nasturtiums, the climbing
Roses, to straighten
Carnations, red
Chrysanthemums; the stiff
Stems, jointed like corn,
They tied and tucked,—
These nurses of nobody else.
Quicker than birds, they dipped
Up and sifted the dirt;
They sprinkled and shook;
They stood astride pipes,
Their skirts billowing out wide into tents,
Their hands twinkling with wet;

Like witches they flew along rows
Keeping creation at ease;
With a tendril for needle
They sewed up the air with a stem;
They teased out the seed that the cold kept asleep,—
All the coils, loops, and whorls.
They trellised the sun; they plotted for more than
        themselves.

I remember how they picked me up, a spindly kid,
Pinching and poking my thin ribs
Till I lay in their laps, laughing,
Weak as a whiffet;
Now, when I'm alone and cold in my bed,
They still hover over me,
These ancient leathery crones,
With their bandannas stiffened with sweat,
And their thorn-bitten wrists,
And their snuff-laden breath blowing lightly over me in
        my first sleep.

Transplanting

Watching hands transplanting,
Turning and tamping,
Lifting the young plants with two fingers,
Sifting in a palm-full of fresh loam,—
One swift movement,—
Then plumping in the bunched roots,

A single twist of the thumbs, a tamping and turning,
All in one,
Quick on the wooden bench,
A shaking down, while the stem stays straight,
Once, twice, and a faint third thump,—
Into the flat-box it goes,
Ready for the long days under the sloped glass:

The sun warming the fine loam,
The young horns winding and unwinding,
Creaking their thin spines,
The underleaves, the smallest buds
Breaking into nakedness,
The blossoms extending
Out into the sweet air,
The whole flower extending outward,
Stretching and reaching.

Child on Top of a Greenhouse

The wind billowing out the seat of my britches,
My feet crackling splinters of glass and dried putty,
The half-grown chrysanthemums staring up like
    accusers,
Up through the streaked glass, flashing with sunlight,
A few white clouds all rushing eastward,
A line of elms plunging and tossing like horses,
And everyone, everyone pointing up and shouting!

Flower Dump

Cannas shiny as slag,
Slug-soft stems,
Whole beds of bloom pitched on a pile,
Carnations, verbenas, cosmos,
Molds, weeds, dead leaves,
Turned-over roots
With bleached veins
Twined like fine hair,
Each clump in the shape of a pot;
Everything limp
But one tulip on top,
One swaggering head
Over the dying, the newly dead.

Carnations

Pale blossoms, each balanced on a single jointed stem,
The leaves curled back in elaborate Corinthian scrolls;
And the air cool, as if drifting down from wet hemlocks,
Or rising out of ferns not far from water,
A crisp hyacinthine coolness,
Like that clear autumnal weather of eternity,
The windless perpetual morning above a September
    cloud.

My Papa's Waltz

The whiskey on your breath
Could make a small boy dizzy;
But I hung on like death:
Such waltzing was not easy.

We romped until the pans
Slid from the kitchen shelf;
My mother's countenance
Could not unfrown itself.

The hand that held my wrist
Was battered on one knuckle;
At every step you missed
My right ear scraped a buckle.

You beat time on my head
With a palm caked hard by dirt,
Then waltzed me off to bed
Still clinging to your shirt.

Pickle Belt

The fruit rolled by all day.
They prayed the cogs would creep;
They thought about Saturday pay,
And Sunday sleep.

Whatever he smelled was good:
The fruit and flesh smells mixed.
There beside him she stood,—
And he, perplexed;

He, in his shrunken britches,
Eyes rimmed with pickle dust,
Prickling with all the itches
Of sixteen-year-old lust.

Dolor

I have known the inexorable sadness of pencils,
Neat in their boxes, dolor of pad and paper-weight,
All the misery of manilla folders and mucilage,
Desolation in immaculate public places,
Lonely reception room, lavatory, switchboard,
The unalterable pathos of basin and pitcher,
Ritual of multigraph, paper-clip, comma,
Endless duplication of lives and objects.
And I have seen dust from the walls of institutions,
Finer than flour, alive, more dangerous than silica,
Sift, almost invisible, through long afternoons of
      tedium,
Dropping a fine film on nails and delicate eyebrows,
Glazing the pale hair, the duplicate gray standard faces.

Double Feature

With Buck still tied to the log, on comes the light.
Lovers disengage, move sheepishly toward the aisle
With mothers, sleep-heavy children, stale perfume, past
    the manager's smile
Out through the velvety chains to the cool air of night.

I dawdle with groups near the rickety pop-corn stand;
Dally at shop windows, still reluctant to go;
I teeter, heels hooked on the curb, scrape a toe;
Or send off a car with vague lifts of a hand.

A wave of Time hangs motionless on this particular
    shore.
I notice a tree, arsenical grey in the light, or the slow
Wheel of the stars, the Great Bear glittering colder than
    snow,
And remember there was something else I was hoping
    for.

The Return

I circled on leather paws
In the darkening corridor,
Crouched closer to the floor,
Then bristled like a dog.

As I turned for a backward look,
The muscles in one thigh
Sagged like a frightened lip.

A cold key let me in
That self-infected lair;
And I lay down with my life,
With the rags and rotting clothes,
With a stump of scraggy fang
Bared for a hunter's boot.

Night Crow

When I saw that clumsy crow
Flap from a wasted tree,
A shape in the mind rose up:
Over the gulfs of dream
Flew a tremendous bird
Further and further away
Into a moonless black,
Deep in the brain, far back.

River Incident

A shell arched under my toes,
Stirred up a whirl of silt
That riffled around my knees.

Whatever I owed to time
Slowed in my human form;
Sea water stood in my veins,
The elements I kept warm
Crumbled and flowed away,
And I knew I had been there before,
In that cold, granitic slime,
In the dark, in the rolling water.

The Minimal

I study the lives on a leaf: the little
Sleepers, numb nudgers in cold dimensions,
Beetles in caves, newts, stone-deaf fishes,
Lice tethered to long limp subterranean weeds,
Squirmers in bogs,
And bacterial creepers
Wriggling through wounds
Like elvers in ponds,
Their wan mouths kissing the warm sutures,
Cleaning and caressing,
Creeping and healing.

The Waking

I strolled across
An open field;
The sun was out;
Heat was happy.

This way! This way!
The wren's throat shimmered,
Either to other,
The blossoms sang.

The stones sang,
The little ones did,
And flowers jumped
Like small goats.

A ragged fringe
Of daisies waved;
I wasn't alone
In a grove of apples.

Far in the wood
A nestling sighed;
The dew loosened
Its morning smells.

I came where the river
Ran over stones:
My ears knew
An early joy.

And all the waters
Of all the streams
Sang in my veins
That summer day.

The Lost Son

    1   *The Flight*

At Woodlawn I heard the dead cry:
I was lulled by thc slamming of iron,
A slow drip over stones,
Toads brooding in wells.
All the leaves stuck out their tongues;
I shook the softening chalk of my bones,
Saying,
Snail, snail, glister me forward,
Bird, soft-sigh me home.
Worm, be with me.
This is my hard time.

Fished in an old wound,
The soft pond of repose;
Nothing nibbled my line,
Not even the minnows came.

Sat in an empty house
Watching shadows crawl,
Scratching.
There was one fly.

Voice, come out of the silence.
Say something.
Appear in the form of a spider
Or a moth beating the curtain.

Tell me:
Which is the way I take;
Out of what door do I go,
Where and to whom?

> Dark hollows said, lee to the wind,
> The moon said, back of an eel,
> The salt said, look by the sea,
> Your tears are not enough praise,
> You will find no comfort here,
> In the kingdom of bang and blab.

Running lightly over spongy ground,
Past the pasture of flat stones,
The three elms,
The sheep strewn on a field,
Over a rickety bridge
Toward the quick-water, wrinkling and rippling.

Hunting along the river,
Down among the rubbish, the bug-riddled foliage,
By the muddy pond-edge, by the bog-holes,
By the shrunken lake, hunting, in the heat of summer.

The shape of a rat?
> It's bigger than that,
> It's less than a leg
> And more than a nose,
> Just under the water
> It usually goes.

Is it soft like a mouse?
Can it wrinkle its nose?
Could it come in the house
On the tips of its toes?

> Take the skin of a cat
> And the back of an eel,
> Then roll them in grease,—
> That's the way it would feel.

> It's sleek as an otter
> With wide webby toes
> Just under the water
> It usually goes.

2   *The Pit*

Where do the roots go?
   Look down under the leaves.
Who put the moss there?
   These stones have been here too long.
Who stunned the dirt into noise?
   Ask the mole, he knows.
I feel the slime of a wet nest.
   Beware Mother Mildew.
Nibble again, fish nerves.

3   *The Gibber*

At the wood's mouth,
By the cave's door,
I listened to something
I had heard before.

Dogs of the groin
Barked and howled,
The sun was against me,
The moon would not have me.

The weeds whined,
The snakes cried,
The cows and briars
Said to me: Die.

What a small song. What slow clouds. What dark water.
Hath the rain a father? All the caves are ice. Only the
    snow's here.
I'm cold. I'm cold all over. Rub me in father and
    mother.
Fear was my father, Father Fear.
His look drained the stones.

    What gliding shape
    Beckoning through halls,
    Stood poised on the stair,
    Fell dreamily down?

    From the mouths of jugs
    Perched on many shelves,
    I saw substance flowing
    That cold morning.

    Like a slither of eels
    That watery cheek
    As my own tongue kissed
    My lips awake.

Is this the storm's heart? The ground is unstilling itself.
My veins are running nowhere. Do the bones cast out
     their fire?
Is the seed leaving the old bed? These buds are live as
     birds.
Where, where are the tears of the world?
Let the kisses resound, flat like a butcher's palm;
Let the gestures freeze; our doom is already decided.
All the windows are burning! What's left of my life?
I want the old rage, the lash of primordial milk!
Good-bye, good-bye, old stones, the time-order is
     going,
I have married my hands to perpetual agitation,
I run, I run to the whistle of money.

    Money money money
    Water water water

How cool the grass is.
Has the bird left?
The stalk still sways.
Has the worm a shadow?
What do the clouds say?

These sweeps of light undo me.
Look, look, the ditch is running white!
I've more veins than a tree!
Kiss me, ashes, I'm falling through a dark swirl.

4   *The Return*

The way to the boiler was dark,
Dark all the way,
Over slippery cinders
Through the long greenhouse.

The roses kept breathing in the dark.
They had many mouths to breathe with.
My knees made little winds underneath
Where the weeds slept.

There was always a single light
Swinging by the fire-pit,
Where the fireman pulled out roses,
The big roses, the big bloody clinkers.

Once I stayed all night.
The light in the morning came slowly over the
    white
Snow.
There were many kinds of cool
Air.
Then came steam.

Pipe-knock.

Scurry of warm over small plants.
Ordnung! Ordnung!
Papa is coming!

A fine haze moved off the leaves;
Frost melted on far panes;
The rose, the chrysanthemum turned toward the
     light.
Even the hushed forms, the bent yellowy weeds
Moved in a slow up-sway.

5   (*It was beginning winter.*)

It was beginning winter,
An in-between time,
The landscape still partly brown:
The bones of weeds kept swinging in the wind,
Above the blue snow.

It was beginning winter.
The light moved slowly over the frozen field,
Over the dry seed-crowns,
The beautiful surviving bones
Swinging in the wind.

Light traveled over the field;
Stayed.
The weeds stopped swinging.
The mind moved, not alone,
Through the clear air, in the silence.

Was it light?
Was it light within?
Was it light within light?
Stillness becoming alive,
Yet still?

A lively understandable spirit
Once entertained you.
It will come again.
Be still.
Wait.

The Long Alley

1

A river glides out of the grass. A river or a serpent.
A fish floats belly upward,
Sliding through the white current,
Slowly turning,
Slowly.

The dark flows on itself. A dead mouth sings under an
     old tree.
The ear hears only in low places.
Remember an old sound.
Remember
Water.

This slag runs slow. What bleeds when metal breaks?
Flesh, you offend this metal. How long need the bones
     mourn?
Are those horns on top of the hill? Yesterday has a long
     look.

Loo, loo, said the sulphurous water,
There's no filth on a plateau of cinders.
This smoke's from the glory of God.

Can you name it? I can't name it.
Let's not hurry. The dead don't hurry.
Who else breathes here? What does the grave say?
My gates are all caves.

2

The fiend's far away. Lord, what do you require?
   The soul resides in the horse barn.
Believe me, there's no one else, kitten-limp sister.
   Kiss the trough, swine-on-Friday.
Come to me, milk-nose. I need a loan of the quick.
   There's no joy in soft bones.
For whom were you made, sweetness I cannot touch?
   Look what the larks do.
Luminous one, shall we meet on the bosom of God?
   Return the gaze of a pond.

3

Stay close. Must I kill something else?
Can feathers eat me? There's no clue in the silt.
This wind gives me scales. Have mercy, gristle:
It's my last waltz with an old itch.

A waiting ghost warms up the dead
Until they creak their knees:
So up and away and what do we do
But barley-break and squeeze.

Tricksy comes and tricksy goes
Bold in fear therefore;
The hay hops in the horse's mouth,
The chin jumps to the nose.

Rich me cherries a fondling's kiss,
The summer bumps of ha:
Hand me a feather, I'll fan you warm,
I'm happy with my paws.

Gilliflower ha,
Gilliflower ho,
My love's locked in
The old silo.
She cries to the hen,
She waves to the goose,
But they don't come
To let her loose.

If we detach
The head of a match
What do we do
To the cat's wish?
Do we rout the fish?
Will the goat's mouth
Have the last laugh?

4

That was a close knock. See what the will wants.
This air could flesh a dead stick. Sweet Jesus, make me
    sweat.

Are the flowers here? The birds are.
Shall I call the flowers?

> Come littlest, come tenderest,
> Come whispering over the small waters,
> Reach me rose, sweet one, still moist in the loam,
> Come, come out of the shade, the cool ways,
> The long alleys of string and stem;
> Bend down, small breathers, creepers and winders;
> Lean from the tiers and benches,
> Cyclamen dripping and lilies.
> What fish-ways you have, littlest flowers,
> Swaying over the walks, in the watery air,
> Drowsing in soft light, petals pulsing.

Light airs! Light airs! A pierce of angels!
The leaves, the leaves become me!
The tendrils have me!

5

Bricks flake before my face. Master of water, that's trees
     away.
Reach me a peach, fondling, the hills are there.
Nuts are money: wherefore and what else?
Send down a rush of air, O torrential,
Make the sea flash in the dust.

Call off the dogs, my paws are gone.
This wind brings many fish;
The lakes will be happy:
Give me my hands:
I'll take the fire.

A Field of Light

1

Came to lakes; came to dead water,
Ponds with moss and leaves floating,
Planks sunk in the sand.

A log turned at the touch of a foot;
A long weed floated upward;
An eye tilted.

> Small winds made
> A chilly noise;
> The softest cove
> Cried for sound.

> Reached for a grape
> And the leaves changed;
> A stone's shape
> Became a clam.

> A fine rain fell
> On fat leaves;
> I was there alone
> In a watery drowse.

2

Angel within me, I asked,
Did I ever curse the sun?
Speak and abide.

Under, under the sheaves,
Under the blackened leaves,
Behind the green viscid trellis,
In the deep grass at the edge of a field,
Along the low ground dry only in August,—

Was it dust I was kissing?
A sigh came far.
Alone, I kissed the skin of a stone;
Marrow-soft, danced in the sand.

3

The dirt left my hand, visitor.
I could feel the mare's nose.
A path went walking.
The sun glittered on a small rapids.
Some morning thing came, beating its wings.
The great elm filled with birds.

Listen, love,
The fat lark sang in the field;
I touched the ground, the ground warmed by the
        killdeer,
The salt laughed and the stones;
The ferns had their ways, and the pulsing lizards,
And the new plants, still awkward in their soil,
The lovely diminutives.

I could watch! I could watch!
I saw the separateness of all things!
My heart lifted up with the great grasses;

The weeds believed me, and the nesting birds.
There were clouds making a rout of shapes crossing a
windbreak of cedars,
And a bee shaking drops from a rain-soaked honeysuckle.
The worms were delighted as wrens.
And I walked, I walked through the light air;
I moved with the morning.

The Shape of the Fire

1

What's this? A dish for fat lips.
Who says? A nameless stranger.
Is he a bird or a tree? Not everyone can tell.

Water recedes to the crying of spiders.
An old scow bumps over black rocks.
A cracked pod calls.

Mother me out of here. What more will the bones
allow?
Will the sea give the wind suck? A toad folds into a
stone.
These flowers are all fangs. Comfort me, fury.
Wake me, witch, we'll do the dance of rotten sticks.

Shale loosens. Marl reaches into the field. Small birds
pass over water.
Spirit, come near. This is only the edge of whiteness.
I can't laugh at a procession of dogs.

In the hour of ripeness, the tree is barren.
The she-bear mopes under the hill.
Mother, mother, stir from your cave of sorrow.

A low mouth laps water. Weeds, weeds, how I love you.
The arbor is cooler. Farewell, farewell, fond worm.
The warm comes without sound.

2

Where's the eye?
The eye's in the sty.
The ear's not here
Beneath the hair.
When I took off my clothes
To find a nose,
There was only one shoe
For the waltz of To,
The pinch of Where.

Time for the flat-headed man. I recognize that listener,
Him with the platitudes and rubber doughnuts,
Melting at the knees, a varicose horror.
Hello, hello. My nerves knew you, dear boy.
Have you come to unhinge my shadow?
Last night I slept in the pits of a tongue.
The silver fish ran in and out of my special bindings;
I grew tired of the ritual of names and the assistant
     keeper of the mollusks:
Up over a viaduct I came, to the snakes and sticks of
     another winter,
A two-legged dog hunting a new horizon of howls.

The wind sharpened itself on a rock;
A voice sang:

> Pleasure on ground
> Has no sound,
> Easily maddens
> The uneasy man.
>
> Who, careless, slips
> In coiling ooze
> Is trapped to the lips,
> Leaves more than shoes;
>
> Must pull off clothes
> To jerk like a frog
> On belly and nose
> From the sucking bog.

My meat eats me. Who waits at the gate?
Mother of quartz, your words writhe into my ear.
Renew the light, lewd whisper.

3

The wasp waits.
   The edge cannot eat the center.
The grape glistens.
   The path tells little to the serpent.
An eye comes out of the wave.
   The journey from flesh is longest.
A rose sways least.
   The redeemer comes a dark way.

Morning-fair, follow me further back
Into that minnowy world of weeds and ditches,
When the herons floated high over the white houses,
And the little crabs slipped into silvery craters.
When the sun for me glinted the sides of a sand grain,
And my intent stretched over the buds at their first
    trembling.

That air and shine: and the flicker's loud summer call:
The bearded boards in the stream and the all of apples;
The glad hen on the hill; and the trellis humming.
Death was not. I lived in a simple drowse:
Hands and hair moved through a dream of wakening
    blossoms.
Rain sweetened the cave and the dove still called;
The flowers leaned on themselves, the flowers in
    hollows;
And love, love sang toward.

5

To have the whole air!
The light, the full sun
Coming down on the flowerheads,
The tendrils turning slowly,
A slow snail-lifting, liquescent;
To be by the rose
Rising slowly out of its bed,
Still as a child in its first loneliness;
To see cyclamen veins become clearer in early sunlight,
And mist lifting out of the brown cattails;

To stare into the after-light, the glitter left on the lake's
     surface,
When the sun has fallen behind a wooded island;
To follow the drops sliding from a lifted oar,
Held up, while the rower breathes, and the small boat
     drifts quietly shoreward;
To know that light falls and fills, often without our
     knowing,
As an opaque vase fills to the brim from a quick
     pouring,
Fills and trembles at the edge yet does not flow over,
Still holding and feeding the stem of the contained
     flower.

Where Knock Is Open Wide

1

A kitten can
Bite with his feet;
Papa and Mamma
Have more teeth.

Sit and play
Under the rocker
Until the cows
All have puppies.

His ears haven't time.
Sing me a sleep-song, please.
A real hurt is soft.

Once upon a tree
I came across a time,
It wasn't even as
A ghoulie in a dream.

There was a mooly man
Who had a rubber hat
And funnier than that,—
He kept it in a can.

What's the time, papa-seed?
Everything has been twice.
My father is a fish.

2

I sing a small sing,
My uncle's away,
He's gone for always,
I don't care either.

I know who's got him,
They'll jump on his belly,
He won't be an angel,
I don't care either.

I know her noise.
Her neck has kittens.
I'll make a hole for her.
In the fire.

Winkie will yellow I sang.
Her eyes went kissing away
It was and it wasn't her there
I sang I sang all day.

3

I know it's an owl. He's making it darker.
Eat where you're at. I'm not a mouse.
Some stones are still warm.
I like soft paws.
Maybe I'm lost,
Or asleep.

A worm has a mouth.
Who keeps me last?
Fish me out.
Please.

God, give me a near. I hear flowers.
A ghost can't whistle.
I know! I know!
Hello happy hands.

4

We went by the river.
Water birds went ching. Went ching.
Stepped in wet. Over stones.
One, his nose had a frog,
But he slipped out.

I was sad for a fish.
Don't hit him on the boat, I said.
Look at him puff. He's trying to talk.
Papa threw him back.

Bullheads have whiskers.
And they bite.

He watered the roses,
His thumb had a rainbow.
The stems said, Thank you.
Dark came early.

That was before. I fell! I fell!
The worm has moved away.
My tears are tired.

Nowhere is out. I saw the cold.
Went to visit the wind. Where the birds die.
How high is have?

I'll be a bite. You be a wink.
Sing the snake to sleep.

> 5
>
> Kisses come back,
> I said to Papa;
> He was all whitey bones
> And skin like paper.
>
> God's somewhere else,
> I said to Mamma.
> The evening came
> A long long time.
>
> I'm somebody else now.
> Don't tell my hands.
> Have I come to always? Not yet.
> One father is enough.
>
> Maybe God has a house.
> But not here.

I Need, I Need

A deep dish. Lumps in it.
I can't taste my mother.
Hoo. I know the spoon.
Sit in my mouth.

A sneeze can't sleep.
Diddle we care
Couldly.

> Went down cellar,
> Talked to a faucet;
> The drippy water
> Had nothing to say.

> Whisper me over,
> Why don't you, begonia,
> There's no alas
> Where I live.

Scratched the wind with a stick.
The leaves liked it.
Do the dead bite?
Mamma, she's a sad fat.

> A dove said dove all day.
> A hat is a house.
> I hid in his.

2

Even steven all is less:
I haven't time for sugar,
Put your finger in your face,
And there will be a booger.

A one is a two is
I know what you is:
You're not very nice,—
So touch my toes twice.

I know you are my nemesis
So bibble where the pebble is.
The Trouble is with No and Yes
As you can see I guess I guess.

I wish I was a pifflebob
I wish I was a funny
I wish I had ten thousand hats,
And made a lot of money.

Open a hole and see the sky:
A duck knows something
You and I don't.
Tomorrow is Friday.

Not you I need.
Go play with your nose.
Stay in the sun,
Snake-eyes.

3

Stop the larks. Can I have my heart back?
Today I saw a beard in a cloud.
The ground cried my name:
Good-bye for being wrong.
Love helps the sun.
But not enough.

4

When you plant, spit in the pot.
A pick likes to hit ice.
Hooray for me and the mice!—
The oats are all right.

Hear me, soft ears and roundy stones!
It's a dear life I can touch.
Who's ready for pink and frisk?
My hoe eats like a goat.

>   Her feet said yes.
>   It was all hay.
>   I said to the gate,
>   Who else knows
>   What water does?
>   Dew ate the fire.

I know another fire.
Has roots.

Praise to the End!

1

It's dark in this wood, soft mocker.
For whom have I swelled like a seed?
What a bone-ache I have.
Father of tensions, I'm down to my skin at last.

It's a great day for the mice.
Prickle-me, tickle-me, close stems.
Bumpkin, he can dance alone.
Ooh, ooh, I'm a duke of eels.

    Arch my back, pretty-bones, I'm dead at both ends.
    Softly softly, you'll wake the clams.
    I'll feed the ghost alone.
    Father, forgive my hands.

The rings have gone from the pond.
The river's alone with its water.
All risings
Fall.

2

Where are you now, my bonny beating gristle,
My blue original dandy, numb with sugar?
Once I fished from the banks, leaf-light and happy:
On the rocks south of quiet, in the close regions of
      kissing,
I romped, lithe as a child, down the summery streets of
      my veins,

Strict as a seed, nippy and twiggy.
Now the water's low. The weeds exceed me.
It's necessary, among the flies and bananas, to keep a
      constant vigil,
For the attacks of false humility take sudden turns for
      the worse.
Lacking the candor of dogs, I kiss the departing air;
I'm untrue to my own excesses.

Rock me to sleep, the weather's wrong.
Speak to me, frosty beard.
Sing to me, sweet.

      Mips and ma the mooly moo,
      The likes of him is biting who,
      A cow's a care and who's a coo?—
      What footie does is final.

      My dearest dear my fairest fair,
      Your father tossed a cat in air,
      Though neither you nor I was there,—
      What footie does is final.

      Be large as an owl, be slick as a frog,
      Be good as a goose, be big as a dog,
      Be sleek as a heifer, be long as a hog,—
      What footie will do will be final.

I conclude! I conclude!
My dearest dust, I can't stay here.
I'm undone by the flip-flap of odious pillows.

An exact fall of waters has rendered me impotent.
I've been asleep in a bower of dead skin.
It's a piece of a prince I ate.
This salt can't warm a stone.
These lazy ashes.

3

The stones were sharp,
The wind came at my back;
Walked along the highway,
Mincing like a cat.

The sun came out;
The lake turned green;
Romped upon the goldy grass,
Aged thirteen.

The sky cracked open
The world I knew;
Lay like the cats do
Sniffing the dew.

I dreamt I was all bones;
The dead slept in my sleeve;
Sweet Jesus tossed me back:
I wore the sun with ease.

The several sounds were low;
The river ebbed and flowed:
Desire was winter-calm,
A moon away.

Such owly pleasures! Fish come first, sweet bird.
Skin's the least of me. Kiss this.
Is the eternal near, fondling?
I hear the sound of hands.

Can the bones breathe? This grave has an ear.
It's still enough for the knock of a worm.

I feel more than a fish.
Ghost, come closer.

4

Arch of air, my heart's original knock,
I'm awake all over:
I've crawled from the mire, alert as a saint or a dog;
I know the back-stream's joy, and the stone's eternal
        pulseless longing.
Felicity I cannot hoard.
My friend, the rat in the wall, brings me the clearest
        messages;
I bask in the bower of change;
The plants wave me in, and the summer apples;
My palm-sweat flashes gold;
Many astounds before, I lost my identity to a pebble;
The minnows love me, and the humped and spitting
        creatures.

I believe! I believe!—
In the sparrow, happy on gravel;
In the winter-wasp, pulsing its wings in the sunlight;
I have been somewhere else; I remember the sea-faced
        uncles.

I hear, clearly, the heart of another singing,
Lighter than bells,
Softer than water.

Wherefore, O birds and small fish, surround me.
Lave me, ultimate waters.
The dark showed me a face.
My ghosts are all gay.
The light becomes me.

Unfold! Unfold!

1

By snails, by leaps of frog, I came here, spirit.
Tell me, body without skin, does a fish sweat?
I can't crawl back through those veins,
I ache for another choice.
The cliffs! The cliffs! They fling me back.
Eternity howls in the last crags,
The field is no longer simple:
It's a soul's crossing time.
The dead speak noise.

2

It's time you stood up and asked
     —Or sat down and did.
A tongue without song
     —Can still whistle in a jug.

You're blistered all over
                    —Who cares? The old owl?
When you find the wind
                    —Look for the white fire.

3

What a whelm of proverbs, Mr. Pinch!
Are the entrails clear, immaculate cabbage?
The last time I nearly whispered myself away.
I was far back, farther than anybody else.
On the jackpine plains I hunted the bird nobody knows;
Fishing, I caught myself behind the ears.
Alone, in a sleep-daze, I stared at billboards;
I was privy to oily fungus and the algae of standing
        waters;
Honored, on my return, by the ancient fellowship of
        rotten stems.
I was pure as a worm on a leaf; I cherished the mold's
        children.
Beetles sweetened my breath.
I slept like an insect.

I met a collector of string, a shepherd of slow forms.
My mission became the salvation of minnows.
I stretched like a board, almost a tree.
Even thread had a speech.

Later, I did and I danced in the simple wood.
A mouse taught me how, I was a happy asker.
Quite-by-chance brought me many cookies.
I jumped in butter.
Hair had kisses.

4

Easy the life of the mouth. What a lust for ripeness!
All openings praise us, even oily holes.
The bulb unravels. Who's floating? Not me.
The eye perishes in the small vision.
What else has the vine loosened?
I hear a dead tongue halloo.

5

Sing, sing, you symbols! All simple creatures,
All small shapes, willow-shy,
In the obscure haze, sing!

A light song comes from the leaves.
A slow sigh says yes. And light sighs;
A low voice, summer-sad.
Is it you, cold father? Father,
For whom the minnows sang?

> A house for wisdom; a field for revelation.
> Speak to the stones, and the stars answer.
> At first the visible obscures:
> Go where light is.

This fat can't laugh.
Only my salt has a chance.
I'll seek my own meekness.
What grace I have is enough.
The lost have their own pace.
The stalks ask something else.
What the grave says,
The nest denies.

In their harsh thickets
The dead thrash.
They help.

I Cry, Love! Love!

1

Went weeping, little bones. But where?
Wasps come when I ask for pigeons.
The sister sands, they slipper soft away.
What else can befall?

    Delight me otherly, white spirit,—
    Some errand, obscure as the wind's circuit,
    A secret to jerk from the lips of a fish.
    Is circularity such a shame?
    A cat goes wider.

What's a thick? Two-by-two's a shape.
This toad could waltz on a drum;
I hear a most lovely huzza:
I'm king of the boops!

2

Reason? That dreary shed, that hutch for grubby
    schoolboys!
The hedgewren's song says something else.
I care for a cat's cry and the hugs, live as water.
I've traced these words in sand with a vestigial tail;

Now the gills are beginning to cry.
Such a sweet noise: I can't sleep for it.
Bless me and the maze I'm in!
Hello, thingy spirit.

    Mouse, mouse, come out of the ferns,
    And small mouths, stay your aimless cheeping:
    A lapful of apples sleeps in this grass.
    That anguish of concreteness!—
    The sun playing on loam,
    And the first dust of spring listing over backlots,—
    I proclaim once more a condition of joy.
    Walk into the wind, willie!

In a sodden place, all raps and knocks approve.
A dry cry comes from my own desert;
The bones are lonely.
Beginnings start without shade,
Thinner than minnows.
The live grass whirls with the sun,
Feet run over the simple stones,
There's time enough.
Behold, in the lout's eye,
Love.

3

I hear the owls, the soft callers, coming down from the
    hemlocks.
The bats weave in and out of the willows,
Wing-crooked and sure,

Downward and upward,
Dipping and veering close to the motionless water.

A fish jumps, shaking out flakes of moonlight.
A single wave starts lightly and easily shoreward,
Wrinkling between reeds in shallower water,
Lifting a few twigs and floating leaves,
Then washing up over small stones.

The shine on the face of the lake
Tilts, backward and forward.
The water recedes slowly,
Gently rocking.

Who untied the tree? I remember now.
We met in a nest. Before I lived.
The dark hair sighed.
We never enter
Alone.

O, Thou Opening, O

1

I'll make it; but it may take me.
The rat's my phase.
My left side's tender.
Read me the stream.

Dazzle me, dizzy aphorist.
Fling me a precept.
I'm a draft sleeping by a stick;
I'm lost in what I have.

> *The Depth calls to the Height*
> *—Neither knows it.*
> *Those close to the Ground*
> *—Only stay out of the Wind.*

Thrum-thrum, who can be equal to ease?
I've seen my father's face before
Deep in the belly of a thing to be.
The Devil isn't dead; he's just away.

Where's Ann? Where's Lou? Where's Jock-with-the-
   Wind?
Forgive me a minute, nymph.
I'll change the image, and my shoes.
A true mole wanders like a worm.

2

And now are we to have that pelludious Jesus-shimmer over all things, the animal's candid gaze, a shade less than feathers, light's broken speech revived, a ghostly going of tame bears, a bright moon on gleaming skin, a thing you cannot say to whisper and equal a Wound?

I'm tired of all that, Bag-Foot. I can hear small angels anytime. Who cares about the dance of dead underwear, or the sad waltz of paper bags? Who ever said God sang in your fat shape? You're not the only keeper of hay. That's a spratling's prattle. And don't be thinking you're simplicity's sweet thing, either. A leaf could drag you.

Where's the great rage of a rocking heart, the high rare true dangerous indignation? Let me persuade more slowly:

> *The dark has its own light.*
> *A son has many fathers.*
> *Stand by a slow stream:*
> *Hear the sigh of what is.*
> *Be a pleased rock*
> *On a plain day.*
> *Waking's*
> *Kissing.*
> *Yes.*

3

You mean?—
I can leap, true to the field,
In the lily's sovereign right?
Be a body lighted with love,
Sad, in a singing-time?
Or happy, correct as a hat?

Oh, what a webby wonder I am!
Swaying, would you believe,
Like a sapling tree,
Enough to please a cloud!

This frog's had another fall.
The old stalk still has a pulse;
I've crept from a cry.
The holy root wags the tail of a hill;
I'm true to soup, and happy to ask:
I sing the green, and things to come,
I'm king of another condition,
So alive I could die!
The ground's beating like flame!
You fat unnecessary hags,
You enemies of skin,—
A dolphin's at my door!
I'm twinkling like a twig!
The lark's my heart!
I'm wild with news!
My fancy's white!
I am my faces,
Love.

Who reads in bed
*   —Fornicates on the stove.*
An old dog
*   —Should sleep on his paws.*

See what the sweet harp says.
Should a song break a sleep?
The round home of a root,—
Is that the place to go?
I'm a tune dying
On harsh stone.
An Eye says,
Come.

I keep dreaming of bees.
This flesh has airy bones,
Going is knowing.
I see; I seek;
I'm near.
Be true,
Skin.

A Light Breather

The spirit moves,
Yet stays:
Stirs as a blossom stirs,
Still wet from its bud-sheath,
Slowly unfolding,
Turning in the light with its tendrils;
Plays as a minnow plays,
Tethered to a limp weed, swinging,
Tail around, nosing in and out of the current,
Its shadows loose, a watery finger;
Moves, like the snail,
Still inward,
Taking and embracing its surroundings,
Never wishing itself away,
Unafraid of what it is,
A music in a hood,
A small thing,
Singing.

Elegy for Jane

My Student, Thrown by a Horse

I remember the neckcurls, limp and damp as tendrils;
And her quick look, a sidelong pickerel smile;
And how, once startled into talk, the light syllables
        leaped for her,
And she balanced in the delight of her thought,
A wren, happy, tail into the wind,
Her song trembling the twigs and small branches.
The shade sang with her;
The leaves, their whispers turned to kissing;
And the mold sang in the bleached valleys under the
        rose.

Oh, when she was sad, she cast herself down into such a
        pure depth,
Even a father could not find her:
Scraping her cheek against straw;
Stirring the clearest water.

My sparrow, you are not here,
Waiting like a fern, making a spiny shadow.
The sides of wet stones cannot console me,
Nor the moss, wound with the last light.

If only I could nudge you from this sleep,
My maimed darling, my skittery pigeon.
Over this damp grave I speak the words of my love:
I, with no rights in this matter,
Neither father nor lover.

The Dance

Is that dance slowing in the mind of man
That made him think the universe could hum?
The great wheel turns its axle when it can;
I need a place to sing, and dancing-room,
And I have made a promise to my ears
I'll sing and whistle romping with the bears.

For they are all my friends: I saw one slide
Down a steep hillside on a cake of ice,—
Or was that in a book? I think with pride:
A caged bear rarely does the same thing twice
In the same way: O watch his body sway!—
This animal remembering to be gay.

I tried to fling my shadow at the moon,
The while my blood leaped with a wordless song.
Though dancing needs a master, I had none
To teach my toes to listen to my tongue.
But what I learned there, dancing all alone,
Was not the joyless motion of a stone.

I take this cadence from a man named Yeats;
I take it, and I give it back again:
For other tunes and other wanton beats
Have tossed my heart and fiddled through my brain.
Yes, I was dancing-mad, and how
That came to be the bears and Yeats would know.

The Waking

I wake to sleep, and take my waking slow.
I feel my fate in what I cannot fear.
I learn by going where I have to go.

We think by feeling. What is there to know?
I hear my being dance from ear to ear.
I wake to sleep, and take my waking slow.

Of those so close beside me, which are you?
God bless the Ground! I shall walk softly there,
And learn by going where I have to go.

Light takes the Tree; but who can tell us how?
The lowly worm climbs up a winding stair;
I wake to sleep, and take my waking slow.

Great Nature has another thing to do
To you and me; so take the lively air,
And, lovely, learn by going where to go.

This shaking keeps me steady. I should know.
What falls away is always. And is near.
I wake to sleep, and take my waking slow.
I learn by going where I have to go.

Words for the Wind

1

Love, love, a lily's my care,
She's sweeter than a tree.
Loving, I use the air
Most lovingly: I breathe;
Mad in the wind I wear
Myself as I should be,
All's even with the odd,
My brother the vine is glad.

Are flower and seed the same?
What do the great dead say?
Sweet Phoebe, she's my theme:
She sways whenever I sway.
"O love me while I am,
You green thing in my way!"
I cried, and the birds came down
And made my song their own.

Motion can keep me still:
She kissed me out of thought
As a lovely substance will;
She wandered; I did not:
I stayed, and light fell

Across her pulsing throat;
I stared, and a garden stone
Slowly became the moon.

The shallow stream runs slack;
The wind creaks slowly by;
Out of a nestling's beak
Comes a tremulous cry
I cannot answer back;
A shape from deep in the eye—
That woman I saw in a stone—
Keeps pace when I walk alone.

2

The sun declares the earth;
The stones leap in the stream;
On a wide plain, beyond
The far stretch of a dream,
A field breaks like the sea;
The wind's white with her name,
And I walk with the wind.

The dove's my will today.
She sways, half in the sun:
Rose, easy on a stem,
One with the sighing vine,
One to be merry with,
And pleased to meet the moon.
She likes wherever I am.

Passion's enough to give
Shape to a random joy:
I cry delight: I know

The root, the core of a cry.
Swan-heart, arbutus-calm,
She moves when time is shy:
Love has a thing to do.

A fair thing grows more fair;
The green, the springing green
Makes an intenser day
Under the rising moon;
I smile, no mineral man;
I bear, but not alone,
The burden of this joy.

3

Under a southern wind,
The birds and fishes move
North, in a single stream;
The sharp stars swing around;
I get a step beyond
The wind, and there I am,
I'm odd and full of love.

Wisdom, where is it found?—
Those who embrace, believe.
Whatever was, still is,
Says a song tied to a tree.
Below, on the ferny ground,
In rivery air, at ease,
I walk with my true love.

What time's my heart? I care.
I cherish what I have
Had of the temporal:

I am no longer young
But the winds and waters are;
What falls away will fall;
All things bring me to love.

4

The breath of a long root,
The shy perimeter
Of the unfolding rose,
The green, the altered leaf,
The oyster's weeping foot,
And the incipient star—
Are part of what she is.
She wakes the ends of life.

Being myself, I sing
The soul's immediate joy.
Light, light, where's my repose?
A wind wreathes round a tree.
A thing is done: a thing
Body and spirit know
When I do what she does:
Creaturely creature, she!—

I kiss her moving mouth,
Her swart hilarious skin;
She breaks my breath in half;
She frolics like a beast;
And I dance round and round,
A fond and foolish man,
And see and suffer myself
In another being, at last.

I Knew a Woman

I knew a woman, lovely in her bones,
When small birds sighed, she would sigh back at them;
Ah, when she moved, she moved more ways than one:
The shapes a bright container can contain!
Of her choice virtues only gods should speak,
Or English poets who grew up on Greek
(I'd have them sing in chorus, cheek to cheek).

How well her wishes went! She stroked my chin,
She taught me Turn, and Counter-turn, and Stand;
She taught me Touch, that undulant white skin;
I nibbled meekly from her proffered hand;
She was the sickle; I, poor I, the rake,
Coming behind her for her pretty sake
(But what prodigious mowing we did make).

Love likes a gander, and adores a goose:
Her full lips pursed, the errant note to seize;
She played it quick, she played it light and loose;
My eyes, they dazzled at her flowing knees;
Her several parts could keep a pure repose,
Or one hip quiver with a mobile nose
(She moved in circles, and those circles moved).

Let seed be grass, and grass turn into hay:
I'm martyr to a motion not my own;
What's freedom for? To know eternity.
I swear she cast a shadow white as stone.
But who would count eternity in days?
These old bones live to learn her wanton ways:
(I measure time by how a body sways).

The Sententious Man

1

Spirit and nature beat in one breast-bone—
I saw a virgin writhing in the dirt—
The serpent's heart sustains the loveless stone:
My indirection found direction out.

Pride in fine lineaments precedes a fall;
True lechers love the flesh, and that is all.

2

We did not fly the flesh. Who does, when young?
A fire leaps on itself: I know that flame.
Some rages save us. Did I rage too long?
The spirit knows the flesh it must consume.

The dream's an instant that calls up her face.
She changed me ice to fire, and fire to ice.

3

Small waves repeat the mind's slow sensual play.
I stay alive, both in and out of time,
By listening to the spirit's smallest cry;
In the long night, I rest within her name—

As if a lion knelt to kiss a rose,
Astonished into passionate repose.

4

Though all's in motion, who is passing by?
The after-image never stays the same.
There was a thicket where I went to die,
And there I thrashed, my thighs and face aflame.

But my least motion changed into a song,
And all dimensions quivered to one thing.

5

An exultation takes us outside life:
I can delight in my own hardihood;
I taste my sister when I kiss my wife;
I drink good liquor when my luck is good.

A drunkard drinks, and belches in his drink;
Such ardor tames eternity, I think.

6

Is pain a promise? I was schooled in pain,
And found out all I could of all desire;
I weep for what I'm like when I'm alone
In the deep center of the voice and fire.

I know the motion of the deepest stone.
Each one's himself, yet each one's everyone.

7

I'm tired of brooding on my neighbor's soul;
My friends become more Christian, year by year.
Small waters run toward a miry hole—
That's not a thing I'm saying with a sneer—

For water moves until it's purified,
And the weak bridegroom strengthens in his bride.

The Pure Fury

1

Stupor of knowledge lacking inwardness—
What book, O learned man, will set me right?
Once I read nothing through a fearful night,
For every meaning had grown meaningless.
Morning, I saw the world with second sight,
As if all things had died, and rose again.
I touched the stones, and they had my own skin.

2

The pure admire the pure, and live alone;
I love a woman with an empty face.
Parmenides put Nothingness in place;
She tries to think, and it flies loose again.
How slow the changes of a golden mean:
Great Boehme rooted all in Yes and No;
At times my darling squeaks in pure Plato.

3

How terrible the need for solitude:
That appetite for life so ravenous
A man's a beast prowling in his own house,
A beast with fangs, and out for his own blood
Until he finds the thing he almost was
When the pure fury first raged in his head
And trees came closer with a denser shade.

4

Dream of a woman, and a dream of death:
The light air takes my being's breath away;
I look on white, and it turns into gray—
When will that creature give me back my breath?
I live near the abyss. I hope to stay
Until my eyes look at a brighter sun
As the thick shade of the long night comes on.

The Surly One

1

When true love broke my heart in half,
I took the whiskey from the shelf,
And told my neighbors when to laugh.
I keep a dog, and bark myself.

2

Ghost cries out to ghost—
But who's afraid of that?
I fear those shadows most
That start from my own feet.

The Beast

I came to a great door,
Its lintel overhung
With burr, bramble, and thorn;
And when it swung, I saw
A meadow, lush and green.

And there a great beast played,
A sportive, aimless one,
A shred of bone its horn,
And colloped round with fern.
It looked at me; it stared.

Swaying, I took its gaze;
Faltered; rose up again;
Rose but to lurch and fall,
Hard, on the gritty sill,
I lay; I languished there.

When I raised myself once more,
The great round eyes had gone.
The long lush grass lay still;
And I wept there, alone.

A Walk in Late Summer

1

A gull rides on the ripples of a dream,
White upon white, slow-settling on a stone;
Across my lawn the soft-backed creatures come;
In the weak light they wander, each alone.
Bring me the meek, for I would know their ways;
I am a connoisseur of midnight eyes.
The small! The small! I hear them singing clear
On the long banks, in the soft summer air.

2

What is there for the soul to understand?
The slack face of the dismal pure inane?
The wind dies down; my will dies with the wind,
God's in that stone, or I am not a man!
Body and soul transcend appearances
Before the caving-in of all that is;
I'm dying piecemeal, fervent in decay;
My moments linger—that's eternity.

3

A late rose ravages the casual eye,
A blaze of being on a central stem.
It lies upon us to undo the lie
Of living merely in the realm of time.
Existence moves toward a certain end—
A thing all earthly lovers understand.
That dove's elaborate way of coming near
Reminds me I am dying with the year.

A tree arises on a central plain—
It is no trick of change or chance of light.
A tree all out of shape from wind and rain,
A tree thinncd by the wind obscures my sight.
The long day dies; I walk the woods alone;
Beyond the ridge two wood thrush sing as one.
Being delights in being, and in time.
The evening wraps me, steady as a flame.

Snake

I saw a young snake glide
Out of the mottled shade
And hang, limp on a stone:
A thin mouth, and a tongue
Stayed, in the still air.

It turned; it drew away;
Its shadow bent in half;
It quickened, and was gone.

I felt my slow blood warm.
I longed to be that thing,
The pure, sensuous form.

And I may be, some time.

Slug

How I loved one like you when I was little!—
With his stripes of silver and his small house on his
    back,
Making a slow journey around the well-curb.
I longed to be like him, and was,
In my way, close cousin
To the dirt, my knees scrubbing
The gravel, my nose wetter than his.

When I slip, just slightly, in the dark,
I know it isn't a wet leaf,
But you, loose toe from the old life,
The cold slime come into being,
A fat, five-inch appendage
Creeping slowly over the wet grass,
Eating the heart out of my garden.

And you refuse to die decently!—
Flying upward through the knives of my lawnmower
Like pieces of smoked eel or raw oyster,
And I go faster in my rage to get done with it,
Until I'm scraping and scratching at you, on the
    doormat,
The small dead pieces sticking under an instep;
Or, poisoned, dragging a white skein of spittle over a
    path—
Beautiful, in its way, like quicksilver—
You shrink to something less,
A rain-drenched fly or spider.

I'm sure I've been a toad, one time or another.
With bats, weasels, worms—I rejoice in the kinship.
Even the caterpillar I can love, and the various vermin.
But as for you, most odious—
Would Blake call you holy?

FROM **Meditations of an Old Woman**

First Meditation

1

On love's worst ugly day,
The weeds hiss at the edge of the field,
The small winds make their chilly indictments.
Elsewhere, in houses, even pails can be sad;
While stones loosen on the obscure hillside,
And a tree tilts from its roots,
Toppling down an embankment.

The spirit moves, but not always upward,
While animals eat to the north,
And the shale slides an inch in the talus,
The bleak wind eats at the weak plateau,
And the sun brings joy to some.
But the rind, often, hates the life within.

How can I rest in the days of my slowness?
I've become a strange piece of flesh,
Nervous and cold, bird-furtive, whiskery,
With a cheek soft as a hound's ear.
What's left is light as a seed;
I need an old crone's knowing.

2

Often I think of myself as riding—
Alone, on a bus through western country.
I sit above the back wheels, where the jolts are hardest,
And we bounce and sway along toward the midnight,
The lights tilting up, skyward, as we come over a little
    rise,
Then down, as we roll like a boat from a wave-crest.

All journeys, I think, are the same:
The movement is forward, after a few wavers,
And for a while we are all alone,
Busy, obvious with ourselves,
The drunken soldier, the old lady with her peppermints;
And we ride, we ride, taking the curves
Somewhat closer, the trucks coming
Down from behind the last ranges,
Their black shapes breaking past;
And the air claps between us,
Blasting the frosted windows,
And I seem to go backward,
Backward in time:

Two song sparrows, one within a greenhouse,
Shuttling its throat while perched on a wind-vent,
And another, outside, in the bright day,
With a wind from the west and the trees all in
    motion.
One sang, then the other,
The songs tumbling over and under the glass,
And the men beneath them wheeling in dirt to the
    cement benches,
The laden wheelbarrows creaking and swaying,
And the up-spring of the plank when a foot left the
    runway.
Journey within a journey:
The ticket mislaid or lost, the gate
Inaccessible, the boat always pulling out
From the rickety wooden dock,
The children waving;
Or two horses plunging in snow, their lines tangled,
A great wooden sleigh careening behind them,
Swerving up a steep embankment.
For a moment they stand above me,
Their black skins shuddering:
Then they lurch forward,
Lunging down a hillside.

3

As when silt drifts and sifts down through muddy
    pond-water
Settling in small beads around weeds and sunken
    branches,
And one crab, tentative, hunches himself before moving
    along the bottom,

Grotesque, awkward, his extended eyes looking at
        nothing in particular,
Only a few bubbles loosening from the ill-matched
        tentacles,
The tail and smaller legs slipping and sliding slowly
        backward—
So the spirit tries for another life,
Another way and place in which to continue;
Or a salmon, tired, moving up a shallow stream,
Nudges into a back-eddy, a sandy inlet,
Bumping against sticks and bottom-stones, then
        swinging
Around, back into the tiny maincurrent, the rush of
        brownish-white water,
Still swimming forward—
So, I suppose, the spirit journeys.

4

I have gone into the waste lonely places
Behind the eye; the lost acres at the edge of smoky
        cities.
What's beyond never crumbles like an embankment,
Explodes like a rose, or thrusts wings over the
        Caribbean.
There are no pursuing forms, faces on walls:
Only the motes of dust in the immaculate hallways,
The darkness of falling hair, the warnings from lint and
        spiders,
The vines graying to a fine powder.
There is no riven tree, or lamb dropped by an eagle.

There are still times, morning and evening:
The cerulean, high in the elm,
Thin and insistent as a cicada,
And the far phoebe, singing,
The long plaintive notes floating down,
Drifting through leaves, oak and maple,
Or the whippoorwill, along the smoky ridges,
A single bird calling and calling;
A fume reminds me, drifting across wet gravel;
A cold wind comes over stones;
A flame, intense, visible,
Plays over the dry pods,
Runs fitfully along the stubble,
Moves over the field,
Without burning.
      In such times, lacking a god,
      I am still happy.

North American Sequence

The Longing

I

On things asleep, no balm:
A kingdom of stinks and sighs,
Fetor of cockroaches, dead fish, petroleum,
Worse than castoreum of mink or weasels,
Saliva dripping from warm microphones,
Agony of crucifixion on barstools.
    Less and less the illuminated lips,
    Hands active, eyes cherished;
    Happiness left to dogs and children—
    (Matters only a saint mentions!)
Lust fatigues the soul.
How to transcend this sensual emptiness?
(Dreams drain the spirit if we dream too long.)
In a bleak time, when a week of rain is a year,
The slag-heaps fume at the edge of the raw cities:
The gulls wheel over their singular garbage;
The great trees no longer shimmer;
Not even the soot dances.

And the spirit fails to move forward,
But shrinks into a half-life, less than itself,

Falls back, a slug, a loose worm
Ready for any crevice,
An eyeless starter.

      II

A wretch needs his wretchedness. Yes.
O pride, thou art a plume upon whose head?

How comprehensive that felicity! . . .
A body with the motion of a soul.
What dream's enough to breathe in? A dark dream.
The rose exceeds, the rose exceeds us all.
Who'd think the moon could pare itself so thin?
A great flame rises from the sunless sea;
The light cries out, and I am there to hear—
I'd be beyond; I'd be beyond the moon,
Bare as a bud, and naked as a worm.

To this extent I'm a stalk.
      —How free; how all alone.
Out of these nothings
      —All beginnings come.

      III

I would with the fish, the blackening salmon, and the
      mad lemmings,
The children dancing, the flowers widening.
Who sighs from far away?
I would unlearn the lingo of exasperation, all the
      distortions of malice and hatred;
I would believe my pain: and the eye quiet on the
      growing rose;

I would delight in my hands, the branch singing,
      altering the excessive bird;
I long for the imperishable quiet at the heart of form;
I would be a stream, winding between great striated
      rocks in late summer;
A leaf, I would love the leaves, delighting in the
      redolent disorder of this mortal life,
This ambush, this silence,
Where shadow can change into flame,
And the dark be forgotten.
I have left the body of the whale, but the mouth of the
      night is still wide;
On the Bullhead, in the Dakotas, where the eagles eat
      well,
In the country of few lakes, in the tall buffalo grass at
      the base of the clay buttes,
In the summer heat, I can smell the dead buffalo,
The stench of their damp fur drying in the sun,
The buffalo chips drying

      Old men should be explorers?
      I'll be an Indian.
      Ogalala?
      Iroquois.

Meditation at Oyster River

I

Over the low, barnacled, elephant-colored rocks,
Come the first tide-ripples, moving, almost without
      sound, toward me,

Running along the narrow furrows of the shore, the
     rows of dead clam shells;
Then a runnel behind me, creeping closer,
Alive with tiny striped fish, and young crabs climbing in
     and out of the water.

No sound from the bay. No violence.
Even the gulls quiet on the far rocks,
Silent, in the deepening light,
Their cat-mewing over,
Their child-whimpering.

At last one long undulant ripple,
Blue-black from where I am sitting,
Makes almost a wave over a barrier of small stones,
Slapping lightly against a sunken log.
I dabble my toes in the brackish foam sliding forward,
Then retire to a rock higher up on the cliff-side.
The wind slackens, light as a moth fanning a stone:
A twilight wind, light as a child's breath
Turning not a leaf, not a ripple.
The dew revives on the beach-grass;
The salt-soaked wood of a fire crackles;
A fish raven turns on its perch (a dead tree in the
     rivermouth),
Its wings catching a last glint of the reflected sunlight.

    II

The self persists like a dying star,
In sleep, afraid. Death's face rises afresh,
Among the shy beasts, the deer at the salt-lick,

The doe with its sloped shoulders loping across the
    highway,
The young snake, poised in green leaves, waiting for its
    fly,
The hummingbird, whirring from quince-blossom to
    morning-glory—
With these I would be.

And with water: the waves coming forward, without
    cessation,
The waves, altered by sand-bars, beds of kelp,
    miscellaneous driftwood,
Topped by cross-winds, tugged at by sinuous
    undercurrents
The tide rustling in, sliding between the ridges of stone,
The tongues of water, creeping in, quietly.

III

In this hour,
In this first heaven of knowing,
The flesh takes on the pure poise of the spirit,
Acquires, for a time, the sandpiper's insouciance,
The hummingbird's surety, the kingfisher's cunning—
I shift on my rock and I think:
Of the first trembling of a Michigan brook in April,
Over a lip of stone, the tiny rivulet;
And that wrist-thick cascade tumbling from a cleft rock,
Its spray holding a double rain-bow in early morning,
Small enough to be taken in, embraced, by two arms,—
Or the Tittebawasee, in the time between winter and
    spring,

When the ice melts along the edges in early afternoon.
And the midchannel begins cracking and heaving from
     the pressure beneath,
The ice piling high against the iron-bound spiles,
Gleaming, freezing hard again, creaking at midnight—
And I long for the blast of dynamite,
The sudden sucking roar as the culvert loosens its debris
     of branches and sticks,
Welter of tin cans, pails, old bird nests, a child's shoe
     riding a log,
As the piled ice breaks away from the battered spiles,
And the whole river begins to move forward, its bridges
     shaking.

    IV

Now, in this waning of light,
I rock with the motion of morning;
In the cradle of all that is,
I'm lulled into half-sleep
By the lapping of water,
Cries of the sandpiper.
Water's my will, and my way,
And the spirit runs, intermittently,
In and out of the small waves,
Runs with the intrepid shorebirds—
How graceful the small before danger!

In the first of the moon,
All's a scattering,
A shining.

Journey to the Interior

In the long journey out of the self,
There are many detours, washed-out interrupted raw
    places
Where the shale slides dangerously
And the back wheels hang almost over the edge
At the sudden veering, the moment of turning.
Better to hug close, wary of rubble and falling stones.
The arroyo cracking the road, the wind-bitten buttes,
    the canyons,
Creeks swollen in midsummer from the flash-flood
    roaring into the narrow valley.
Reeds beaten flat by wind and rain,
Gray from the long winter, burnt at the base in late
    summer.
—Or the path narrowing,
Winding upward toward the stream with its sharp
    stones,
The upland of alder and birchtrees,
Through the swamp alive with quicksand,
The way blocked at last by a fallen fir-tree,
The thickets darkening,
The ravines ugly.

II

I remember how it was to drive in gravel,
Watching for dangerous down-hill places, where the
    wheels whined beyond eighty—
When you hit the deep pit at the bottom of the swale,

The trick was to throw the car sideways and charge over
the hill, full of the throttle.
Grinding up and over the narrow road, spitting and
roaring.
A chance? Perhaps. But the road was part of me, and its
ditches,
And the dust lay thick on my eyelids,—Who ever wore
goggles?—
Always a sharp turn to the left past a barn close to the
roadside,
To a scurry of small dogs and a shriek of children,
The highway ribboning out in a straight thrust to the
North,
To the sand dunes and fish flies, hanging, thicker than
moths,
Dying brightly under the street lights sunk in coarse
concrete,
The towns with their high pitted road-crowns and deep
gutters,
Their wooden stores of silvery pine and weather-beaten
red courthouses,
An old bridge below with a buckled iron railing, broken
by some idiot plunger;
Underneath, the sluggish water running between weeds,
broken wheels, tires, stones.
And all flows past—
The cemetery with two scrubby trees in the middle of
the prairie,
The dead snakes and muskrats, the turtles gasping in the
rubble,

The spikey purple bushes in the winding dry creek
  bed—
The floating hawks, the jackrabbits, the grazing cattle—
I am not moving but they are,
And the sun comes out of a blue cloud over the Tetons,
While, farther away, the heat-lightning flashes.
I rise and fall in the slow sea of a grassy plain,
The wind veering the car slightly to the right,
Whipping the line of white laundry, bending the
  cottonwoods apart,
The scraggly wind-break of a dusty ranch-house.
I rise and fall, and time folds
Into a long moment;
And I hear the lichen speak,
And the ivy advance with its white lizard feet—
On the shimmering road,
On the dusty detour.

III

I see the flower of all water, above and below me, the
  never receding,
Moving, unmoving in a parched land, white in the
  moonlight:
The soul at a still-stand,
At ease after rocking the flesh to sleep,
Petals and reflections of petals mixed on the surface of a
  glassy pool,
And the waves flattening out when the fishermen drag
  their nets over the stones.

In the moment of time when the small drop forms, but
     does not fall,
I have known the heart of the sun,—
In the dark and light of a dry place,
In a flicker of fire brisked by a dusty wind.
I have heard, in a drip of leaves,
A slight song,
After the midnight cries.
I rehearse myself for this:
The stand at the stretch in the face of death,
Delighting in surface change, the glitter of light on
     waves,
And I roam elsewhere, my body thinking,
Turning toward the other side of light,
In a tower of wind, a tree idling in air,
Beyond my own echo,
Neither forward nor backward,
Unperplexed, in a place leading nowhere.

As a blind man, lifting a curtain, knows it is morning,
I know this change:
On one side of silence there is no smile;
But when I breathe with the birds,
The spirit of wrath becomes the spirit of blessing,
And the dead begin from their dark to sing in my sleep.

The Long Waters

Whether the bees have thoughts, we cannot say,
But the hind part of the worm wiggles the most,
Minnows can hear, and butterflies, yellow and blue,
Rejoice in the language of smells and dancing.
Therefore I reject the world of the dog
Though he hear a note higher than C
And the thrush stopped in the middle of his song.

And I acknowledge my foolishness with God,
My desire for the peaks, the black ravines, the rolling
    mists
Changing with every twist of wind,
The unsinging fields where no lungs breathe,
Where light is stone.
I return where fire has been,
To the charred edge of the sea
Where the yellowish prongs of grass poke through the
    blackened ash,
And the bunched logs peel in the afternoon sunlight,
Where the fresh and salt waters meet,
And the sea-winds move through the pine trees,
A country of bays and inlets, and small streams flowing
    seaward.

II

Mnetha, Mother of Har, protect me
From the worm's advance and retreat, from the
    butterfly's havoc,

From the slow sinking of the island peninsula, the coral
　　efflorescence,
The dubious sea-change, the heaving sands, and my
　　tentacled sea-cousins.

But what of her?—
Who magnifies the morning with her eyes,
That star winking beyond itself,
The cricket-voice deep in the midnight field,
The blue jay rasping from the stunted pine.

How slowly pleasure dies!—
The dry bloom splitting in the wrinkled vale,
The first snow of the year in the dark fir.
Feeling, I still delight in my last fall.

III

In time when the trout and young salmon leap for the
　　low-flying insects,
And the ivy-branch, cast to the ground, puts down roots
　　into the sawdust,
And the pine, whole with its roots, sinks into the
　　estuary,
Where it leans, tilted east, a perch for the osprey,
And a fisherman dawdles over a wooden bridge,
These waves, in the sun, remind me of flowers:
The lily's piercing white,
The mottled tiger, best in the corner of a damp place,
The heliotrope, veined like a fish, the persistent
　　morning-glory,

And the bronze of a dead burdock at the edge of a
     prairie lake,
Down by the muck shrinking to the alkaline center.

I have come here without courting silence,
Blessed by the lips of a low wind,
To a rich desolation of wind and water,
To a landlocked bay, where the salt water is freshened
By small streams running down under fallen fir trees.

    IV

In the vaporous gray of early morning,
Over the thin, feathery ripples breaking lightly against
     the irregular shoreline—
Feathers of the long swell, burnished, almost oily—
A single wave comes in like the neck of a great swan
Swimming slowly, its back ruffled by the light
     cross-winds,
To a tree lying flat, its crown half broken.

I remember a stone breaking the eddying current,
Neither white nor red, in the dead middle way,
Where impulse no longer dictates, nor the darkening
     shadow,
A vulnerable place,
Surrounded by sand, broken shells, the wreckage of
     water.

    V

As light reflects from a lake, in late evening,
When bats fly, close to slightly tilting brownish water,

And the low ripples run over a pebbly shoreline,
As a fire, seemingly long dead, flares up from a
        downdraft of air in a chimney,
Or a breeze moves over the knees from a low hill,
So the sea wind wakes desire.
My body shimmers with a light flame.

I see in the advancing and retreating waters
The shape that came from my sleep, weeping:
The eternal one, the child, the swaying vine branch,
The numinous ring around the opening flower,
The friend that runs before me on the windy headlands,
Neither voice nor vision.

I, who came back from the depths laughing too loudly,
Become another thing;
My eyes extend beyond the farthest bloom of the waves;
I lose and find myself in the long water;
I am gathered together once more;
I embrace the world.

The Far Field

I

I dream of journeys repeatedly:
Of flying like a bat deep into a narrowing tunnel,
Of driving alone, without luggage, out a long peninsula,
The road lined with snow-laden second growth,
A fine dry snow ticking the windshield,
Alternate snow and sleet, no on-coming traffic,

And no lights behind, in the blurred side-mirror,
The road changing from glazed tarface to a rubble of
    stone,
Ending at last in a hopeless sand-rut,
Where the car stalls,
Churning in a snowdrift
Until the headlights darken.

    II

At the field's end, in the corner missed by the mower,
Where the turf drops off into a grass-hidden culvert,
Haunt of the cat-bird, nesting-place of the field-mouse,
Not too far away from the ever-changing flower-dump,
Among the tin cans, tires, rusted pipes, broken
    machinery,—
One learned of the eternal;
And in the shrunken face of a dead rat, eaten by rain and
    ground-beetles
(I found it lying among the rubble of an old coal bin)
And the tom-cat, caught near the pheasant-run,
Its entrails strewn over the half-grown flowers,
Blasted to death by the night watchman.

I suffered for birds, for young rabbits caught in the
    mower,
My grief was not excessive.
For to come upon warblers in early May
Was to forget time and death:
How they filled the oriole's elm, a twittering restless
    cloud, all one morning,

And I watched and watched till my eyes blurred from
    the bird shapes,—
Cape May, Blackburnian, Cerulean,—
Moving, elusive as fish, fearless,
Hanging, bunched like young fruit, bending the end
    branches,
Still for a moment,
Then pitching away in half-flight,
Lighter than finches,
While the wrens bickered and sang in the half-green
    hedgerows,
And the flicker drummed from his dead tree in the
    chicken-yard.

—Or to lie naked in sand,
In the silted shallows of a slow river,
Fingering a shell,
Thinking:
Once I was something like this, mindless,
Or perhaps with another mind, less peculiar;
Or to sink down to the hips in a mossy quagmire;
Or, with skinny knees, to sit astride a wet log,
Believing:
I'll return again,
As a snake or a raucous bird,
Or, with luck, as a lion.

I learned not to fear infinity,
The far field, the windy cliffs of forever,
The dying of time in the white light of tomorrow,

The wheel turning away from itself,
The sprawl of the wave,
The on-coming water.

III

The river turns on itself,
The tree retreats into its own shadow.
I feel a weightless change, a moving forward
As of water quickening before a narrowing channel
When banks converge, and the wide river whitens;
Or when two rivers combine, the blue glacial torrent
And the yellowish-green from the mountainy upland,—
At first a swift rippling between rocks,
Then a long running over flat stones
Before descending to the alluvial plain,
To the clay banks, and the wild grapes hanging from the
      elmtrees,
The slightly trembling water
Dropping a fine yellow silt where the sun stays;
And the crabs bask near the edge,
The weedy edge, alive with small snakes and
      bloodsuckers,—

I have come to a still, but not a deep center,
A point outside the glittering current;
My eyes stare at the bottom of a river,
At the irregular stones, iridescent sandgrains,
My mind moves in more than one place,
In a country half-land, half-water.

I am renewed by death, thought of my death,
The dry scent of a dying garden in September,
The wind fanning the ash of a low fire.
What I love is near at hand,
Always, in earth and air.

IV

The lost self changes,
Turning toward the sea,
A sea-shape turning around,—
An old man with his feet before the fire,
In robes of green, in garments of adieu.

A man faced with his own immensity
Wakes all the waves, all their loose wandering fire.
The murmur of the absolute, the why
Of being born fails on his naked ears.
His spirit moves like monumental wind
That gentles on a sunny blue plateau.
He is the end of things, the final man.

All finite things reveal infinitude:
The mountain with its singular bright shade
Like the blue shine on freshly frozen snow,
The after-light upon ice-burdened pines;
Odor of basswood on a mountain-slope,
A scent beloved of bees;
Silence of water above a sunken tree:
The pure serene of memory in one man,—
A ripple widening from a single stone
Winding around the waters of the world.

The Rose

There are those to whom place is unimportant,
But this place, where sea and fresh water meet,
Is important—
Where the hawks sway out into the wind,
Without a single wingbeat,
And the eagles sail low over the fir trees,
And the gulls cry against the crows
In the curved harbors,
And the tide rises up against the grass
Nibbled by sheep and rabbits.

A time for watching the tide,
For the heron's hieratic fishing,
For the sleepy cries of the towhee,
The morning birds gone, the twittering finches,
But still the flash of the kingfisher, the wingbeat of the
        scoter,
The sun a ball of fire coming down over the water,
The last geese crossing against the reflected afterlight,
The moon retreating into a vague cloud-shape
To the cries of the owl, the eerie whooper.
The old log subsides with the lessening waves,
And there is silence.

I sway outside myself
Into the darkening currents,
Into the small spillage of driftwood,
The waters swirling past the tiny headlands.

Was it here I wore a crown of birds for a moment
While on a far point of the rocks
The light heightened,
And below, in a mist out of nowhere,
The first rain gathered?

II

As when a ship sails with a light wind—
The waves less than the ripples made by rising fish,
The lacelike wrinkles of the wake widening, thinning
    out,
Sliding away from the traveler's eye,
The prow pitching easily up and down,
The whole ship rolling slightly sideways,
The stern high, dipping like a child's boat in a pond—
Our motion continues.

But this rose, this rose in the sea-wind,
Stays,
Stays in its true place,
Flowering out of the dark,
Widening at high noon, face upward,
A single wild rose, struggling out of the white embrace
    of the morning-glory,
Out of the briary hedge, the tangle of matted
    underbrush,
Beyond the clover, the ragged hay,
Beyond the sea pine, the oak, the wind-tipped madrona,
Moving with the waves, the undulating driftwood,
Where the slow creek winds down to the black sand of
    the shore

With its thick grassy scum and crabs scuttling back into
    their glistening craters.

And I think of roses, roses,
White and red, in the wide six-hundred-foot
    greenhouses,
And my father standing astride the cement benches,
Lifting me high over the four-foot stems, the Mrs.
    Russells, and his own elaborate hybrids,
And how those flowerheads seemed to flow toward me,
    to beckon me, only a child, out of myself.
What need for heaven, then,
With that man, and those roses?

III

What do they tell us, sound and silence?
I think of American sounds in this silence:
On the banks of the Tombstone, the wind-harps having
    their say,
The thrush singing alone, that easy bird,
The killdeer whistling away from me,
The mimetic chortling of the catbird
Down in the corner of the garden, among the raggedy
    lilacs,
The bobolink skirring from a broken fencepost,
The bluebird, lover of holes in old wood, lilting its light
    song,
And that thin cry, like a needle piercing the ear, the
    insistent cicada,
And the ticking of snow around oil drums in the
    Dakotas,

The thin whine of telephone wires in the wind of a
      Michigan winter,
The shriek of nails as old shingles are ripped from the
      top of a roof,
The bulldozer backing away, the hiss of the sandblaster,
And the deep chorus of horns coming up from the
      streets in early morning.
I return to the twittering of swallows above water,
And that sound, that single sound,
When the mind remembers all,
And gently the light enters the sleeping soul,
A sound so thin it could not woo a bird,

Beautiful my desire, and the place of my desire.

I think of the rock singing, and light making its own
      silence,
At the edge of a ripening meadow, in early summer,
The moon lolling in the close elm, a shimmer of silver,
Or that lonely time before the breaking of morning
When the slow freight winds along the edge of the
      ravaged hillside,
And the wind tries the shape of a tree,
While the moon lingers,
And a drop of rain water hangs at the tip of a leaf
Shifting in the wakening sunlight
Like the eye of a new-caught fish.

IV

I live with the rock, their weeds,
Their filmy fringes of green, their harsh

Edges, their holes
Cut by the sea-slime, far from the crash
Of the long swell,
The oily, tar-laden walls
Of the toppling waves,
Where the salmon ease their way into the kelp beds,
And the sea rearranges itself among the small islands.

Near this rose, in this grove of sun-parched,
      wind-warped madronas,
Among the half-dead trees, I came upon the true ease of
      myself,
As if another man appeared out of the depths of my
      being,
And I stood outside myself,
Beyond becoming and perishing,
A something wholly other,
As if I swayed out on the wildest wave alive,
And yet was still.
And I rejoiced in being what I was:
In the lilac change, the white reptilian calm,
In the bird beyond the bough, the single one
With all the air to greet him as he flies,
The dolphin rising from the darkening waves;

And in this rose, this rose in the sea-wind,
Rooted in stone, keeping the whole of light,
Gathering to itself sound and silence—
Mine and the sea-wind's.

Elegy

Her face like a rain-beaten stone on the day she rolled
    off
With the dark hearse, and enough flowers for an
    alderman,—
And so she was, in her way, Aunt Tilly.

Sighs, sighs, who says they have sequence?
Between the spirit and the flesh,—what war?
She never knew;
For she asked no quarter and gave none,
Who sat with the dead when the relatives left,
Who fed and tended the infirm, the mad, the epileptic,
And, with a harsh rasp of a laugh at herself,
Faced up to the worst.

I recall how she harried the children away all the late
    summer
From the one beautiful thing in her yard, the peachtree;
How she kept the wizened, the fallen, the misshapen for
    herself,
And picked and pickled the best, to be left on rickety
    doorsteps.

And yet she died in agony,
Her tongue, at the last, thick, black as an ox's.

Terror of cops, bill collectors, betrayers of the poor,—
I see you in some celestial supermarket,

Moving serenely among the leeks and cabbages,
Probing the squash,
Bearing down, with two steady eyes,
On the quaking butcher.

Otto

I

He was the youngest son of a strange brood,
A Prussian who learned early to be rude
To fools and frauds: He does not put on airs
Who lived above a potting shed for years.
I think of him, and I think of his men,
As close to him as any kith or kin.
Max Laurisch had the greenest thumb of all.
A florist does not woo the beautiful:
He potted plants as if he hated them.
What root of his ever denied its stem?
When flowers grew, their bloom extended him.

II

His hand could fit into a woman's glove,
And in a wood he knew whatever moved;
Once when he saw two poachers on his land,
He threw his rifle over with one hand;
Dry bark flew in their faces from his shot,—
He always knew what he was aiming at.
They stood there with their guns; he walked toward,
Without his rifle, and slapped each one hard;

It was no random act, for those two men
Had slaughtered game, and cut young fir trees down.
I was no more than seven at the time.

III

A house for flowers! House upon house they built,
Whether for love or out of obscure guilt
For ancestors who loved a warlike show,
Or Frenchmen killed a hundred years ago,
And yet still violent men, whose stacked-up guns
Killed every cat that neared their pheasant runs;
When Hattie Wright's angora died as well,
My father took it to her, by the tail.
Who loves the small can be both saint and boor,
(And some grow out of shape, their seed impure;)
The Indians loved him, and the Polish poor.

IV

In my mind's eye I see those fields of glass,
As I looked out at them from the high house,
Riding beneath the moon, hid from the moon,
Then slowly breaking whiter in the dawn;
When George the watchman's lantern dropped from
      sight
The long pipes knocked: it was the end of night.
I'd stand upon my bed, a sleepless child
Watching the waking of my father's world.—
O world so far away! O my lost world!

The Meadow Mouse

I

In a shoe box stuffed in an old nylon stocking
Sleeps the baby mouse I found in the meadow,
Where he trembled and shook beneath a stick
Till I caught him up by the tail and brought him in,
Cradled in my hand,
A little quaker, the whole body of him trembling,
His absurd whiskers sticking out like a cartoon-mouse,
His feet like small leaves,
Little lizard-feet,
Whitish and spread wide when he tried to struggle
    away,
Wriggling like a minuscule puppy.

Now he's eaten his three kinds of cheese and drunk
    from his bottle-cap watering-trough—
So much he just lies in one corner,
His tail curled under him, his belly big
As his head; his bat-like ears
Twitching, tilting toward the least sound.

Do I imagine he no longer trembles
When I come close to him?
He seems no longer to tremble.

II

But this morning the shoe-box house on the back porch
    is empty.
Where has he gone, my meadow mouse,

My thumb of a child that nuzzled in my palm?—
To run under the hawk's wing,
Under the eye of the great owl watching from the
    elm-tree,
To live by courtesy of the shrike, the snake, the tom-cat.

I think of the nestling fallen into the deep grass,
The turtle gasping in the dusty rubble of the highway,
The paralytic stunned in the tub, and the water rising,—
All things innocent, hapless, forsaken.

Heard in a Violent Ward

In heaven, too,
You'd be institutionalized.
But that's all right,—
If they let you eat and swear
With the likes of Blake,
And Christopher Smart,
And that sweet man, John Clare.

The Geranium

When I put her out, once, by the garbage pail,
She looked so limp and bedraggled,
So foolish and trusting, like a sick poodle,
Or a wizened aster in late September,

I brought her back in again
For a new routine—
Vitamins, water, and whatever
Sustenance seemed sensible
At the time: she'd lived
So long on gin, bobbie pins, half-smoked cigars, dead
      beer,
Her shriveled petals falling
On the faded carpet, the stale
Steak grease stuck to her fuzzy leaves.
(Dried-out, she creaked like a tulip.)

The things she endured!—
The dumb dames shrieking half the night
Or the two of us, alone, both seedy,
Me breathing booze at her,
She leaning out of her pot toward the window.

Near the end, she seemed almost to hear me—
And that was scary—
So when that snuffling cretin of a maid
Threw her, pot and all, into the trash-can,
I said nothing.

But I sacked the presumptuous hag the next week,
I was that lonely.

The Storm

(Forio d'Ischia)

I

Against the stone breakwater,
Only an ominous lapping,
While the wind whines overhead,
Coming down from the mountain,
Whistling between the arbors, the winding terraces;
A thin whine of wires, a rattling and flapping of leaves,
And the small street-lamp swinging and slamming
      against the lamp-pole.

Where have the people gone?
There is one light on the mountain.

II

Along the sea-wall, a steady sloshing of the swell,
The waves not yet high, but even,
Coming closer and closer upon each other;
A fine fume of rain driving in from the sea,
Riddling the sand, like a wide spray of buckshot,
The wind from the sea and the wind from the mountain
      contending,
Flicking the foam from the whitecaps straight upward
      into the darkness.

A time to go home!—
And a child's dirty shift billows upward out of an alley,
A cat runs from the wind as we do,
Between the whitening trees, up Santa Lucia,

Where the heavy door unlocks,
And our breath comes more easy,—
Then a crack of thunder, and the black rain runs over
     us, over
The flat-roofed houses, coming down in gusts, beating
The walls, the slatted windows, driving
The last watcher indoors, moving the cardplayers closer
To their cards, their anisette.

III

We creep to our bed, and its straw mattress.
We wait; we listen.
The storm lulls off, then redoubles,
Bending the trees half-way down to the ground,
Shaking loose the last wizened oranges in the orchard,
Flattening the limber carnations.

A spider eases himself down from a swaying light-bulb,
Running over the coverlet, down under the iron
     bedstead.
The bulb goes on and off, weakly.
Water roars into the cistern.

We lie closer on the gritty pillow,
Breathing heavily, hoping—
For the great last leap of the wave over the breakwater,
The flat boom on the beach of the towering sea-swell,
The sudden shudder as the jutting sea-cliff collapses,
And the hurricane drives the dead straw into the living
     pine-tree.

The Thing

Suddenly they came flying, like a long scarf of smoke,
Trailing a thing—what was it?—small as a lark
Above the blue air, in the slight haze beyond,
A thing in and out of sight,
Flashing between gold levels of the late sun,
Then throwing itself up and away from the implacable
        swift pursuers,
Confusing them once flying straight into the sun
So they circled aimlessly for almost a minute,
Only to find, with their long terrible eyes
The small thing diving down toward a hill,
Where they dropped again
In one streak of pursuit.

Then the first bird
Struck;
Then another, another,
Until there was nothing left,
Not even feathers from so far away.

And we turned to our picnic
Of veal soaked in marsala and little larks arranged on a
        long platter,
And we drank the dry harsh wine
While I poked with a stick at a stone near a four-pronged
        flower,
And a black bull nudged at a wall in the valley below,
And the blue air darkened.

FROM Sequence, Sometimes Metaphysical

In a Dark Time

In a dark time, the eye begins to see,
I meet my shadow in the deepening shade;
I hear my echo in the echoing wood—
A lord of nature weeping to a tree.
I live between the heron and the wren,
Beasts of the hill and serpents of the den.

What's madness but nobility of soul
At odds with circumstance? The day's on fire!
I know the purity of pure despair,
My shadow pinned against a sweating wall.
That place among the rocks—is it a cave,
Or winding path? The edge is what I have.

A steady storm of correspondences!
A night flowing with birds, a ragged moon,
And in broad day the midnight come again!
A man goes far to find out what he is—
Death of the self in a long, tearless night,
All natural shapes blazing unnatural light.

Dark, dark my light, and darker my desire.
My soul, like some heat-maddened summer fly,
Keeps buzzing at the sill. Which I is *I*?
A fallen man, I climb out of my fear.
The mind enters itself, and God the mind,
And one is One, free in the tearing wind.

The Sequel

I

Was I too glib about eternal things,
An intimate of air and all its songs?
Pure aimlessness pursued and yet pursued
And all wild longings of the insatiate blood
Brought me down to my knees. O who can be
Both moth and flame? The weak moth blundering by.
Whom do we love? I thought I knew the truth;
Of grief I died, but no one knew my death.

II

I saw a body dancing in the wind,
A shape called up out of my natural mind;
I heard a bird stir in its true confine;
A nestling sighed—I called that nestling mine;
A partridge drummed; a minnow nudged its stone;
We danced, we danced, under a dancing moon;
And on the coming of the outrageous dawn,
We danced together, we danced on and on.

III

Morning's a motion in a happy mind:
She stayed in light, as leaves live in the wind,
Swaying in air, like some long water weed.
She left my body, lighter than a seed;
I gave her body full and grave farewell.
A wind came close, like a shy animal.
A light leaf on a tree, she swayed away
To the dark beginnings of another day.

IV

Was nature kind? The heart's core tractable?
All waters waver, and all fires fail.
Leaves, leaves, lean forth and tell me what I am;
This single tree turns into purest flame.
I am a man, a man at intervals
Pacing a room, a room with dead-white walls;
I feel the autumn fail—all that slow fire
Denied in me, who has denied desire.

The Right Thing

Let others probe the mystery if they can.
Time-harried prisoners of *Shall* and *Will*—
The right thing happens to the happy man.

The bird flies out, the bird flies back again;
The hill becomes the valley, and is still;
Let others delve that mystery if they can.

God bless the roots!—Body and soul are one!
The small become the great, the great the small;
The right thing happens to the happy man.

Child of the dark, he can outleap the sun,
His being single, and that being all:
The right thing happens to the happy man.

Or he sits still, a solid figure when
The self-destructive shake the common wall;
Takes to himself what mystery he can,

And, praising change as the slow night comes on,
Wills what he would surrendering his will
Till mystery is no more: No more he can.
The right thing happens to the happy man.

Dinky

O what's the weather in a Beard?
It's windy there, and rather weird,
And when you think the sky has cleared
　—Why, there is Dirty Dinky.

Suppose you walk out in a Storm,
With nothing on to keep you warm,
And then step barefoot on a Worm
　—Of course, it's Dirty Dinky.

As I was crossing a hot hot Plain,
I saw a sight that caused me pain,
You asked me before, I'll tell you again:
　—It *looked* like Dirty Dinky.

Last night you lay a-sleeping?
No! The room was thirty-five below;
The sheets and blankets turned to snow.
　—He'd got in: Dirty Dinky.

You'd better watch the things you do,
You'd better watch the things you do.
You're part of him; he's part of you
　—*You* may be Dirty Dinky.

The Cow

There Once was a Cow with a Double Udder.
When I think of it now, I just have to Shudder!
She was too much for Onc, you can bet your Life:
She had to be Milked by a Man and His Wife.

The Serpent

There was a Serpent who had to sing.
There was. There was.
He simply gave up Serpenting.
Because. Because.

He didn't like his Kind of Life;
He couldn't find a proper Wife;
He was a Serpent with a soul;
He got no Pleasure down his Hole.
And so, of course, he had to Sing,
And sing he did, like Anything!
The Birds, they were, they were Astounded;
And various Measures Propounded
To stop the Serpent's Awful Racket:
They bought a Drum. He wouldn't Whack it.
They sent,—you always send,—to Cuba
And got a Most Commodious Tuba;
They got a Horn, they got a Flute,
But Nothing would suit.
He said, "Look, Birds, all this is futile

I do *not* like to Bang or Tootle."
And then he cut loose with a Horrible Note
That practically split the Top of his Throat.
"You see," he said, with a Serpent's Leer,
"I'm Serious about my Singing Career!"
And the Woods Resounded with many a Shriek
As the Birds flew off to the End of Next Week.

The Sloth

In moving-slow he has no Peer.
You ask him something in his ear;
He thinks about it for a Year;

And, then, before he says a Word
There, upside down (unlike a Bird)
He will assume that you have Heard—

A most Ex-as-per-at-ing Lug.
But should you call his manner Smug,
He'll sigh and give his Branch a Hug;

Then off again to Sleep he goes,
Still swaying gently by his Toes,
And you just *know* he knows he knows.

The Lady and the Bear

A Lady came to a Bear by a Stream.
"O why are you fishing that way?
Tell me, dear Bear there by the Stream,
Why are you fishing that way?"

"I am what is known as a Biddly Bear,—
That's why I'm fishing this way.
We Biddly's are Pee-culiar Bears.
And so,—I'm fishing this way.

And besides, it seems there's a Law:
A most, most exactious Law
Says a Bear
Doesn't dare
Doesn't dare
Doesn't DARE
Use a Hook or a Line,
Or an old piece of Twine,
Not even the end of his Claw, Claw, Claw,
Not even the end of his Claw.
Yes, a Bear has to fish with his Paw, Paw.
A Bear has to fish with his Paw."

"O it's wonderful how with a flick of your Wrist,
You can fish out a fish, out a fish, out a fish,
If *I* were a fish I just couldn't resist
You, when you are fishing that way, that way,
When you are fishing that way."

And at that the Lady slipped from the Bank
And fell in the Stream still clutching a Plank,
But the Bear just sat there until she Sank;
As he went on fishing his way, his way,
As he went on fishing his way.

The Kitty-Cat Bird

The Kitty-Cat Bird, he sat on a Fence.
Said the Wren, your Song isn't worth 10¢.
You're a Fake, you're a Fraud, you're a Hor-rid
          Pretense!
  —Said the Wren to the Kitty-Cat Bird.

You've too many Tunes, and none of them Good:
I wish you would act like a bird really should,
Or stay by yourself down deep in the wood,
  —Said the Wren to the Kitty-Cat Bird.

You mew like a Cat, you grate like a Jay:
You squeak like a Mouse that's lost in the Hay,
I wouldn't be You for even a day,
  —Said the Wren to the Kitty-Cat Bird.

The Kitty-Cat Bird, he moped and he cried.
Then a real cat came with a Mouth so Wide,
That the Kitty-Cat Bird just hopped inside;
"At last I'm myself!"—and he up and died
  —Did the Kitty—the Kitty-Cat Bird.

You'd better not laugh; and don't say, "Pooh!"
Until you have thought this Sad Tale through:
Be sure that whatever you are is you
    —Or you'll end like the Kitty-Cat Bird.

The Whale

There was a most Monstrous Whale:
He had no Skin, he had no Tail.
When he tried to Spout, that Great Big Lubber,
The best he could do was Jiggle his Blubber.

The Yak

There was a most odious Yak
Who took only toads on his Back:
If you asked for a Ride,
He would act very Snide,
And go humping off, yicketty-yak.

The Donkey

I had a Donkey, that was all right,
But he always wanted to fly my Kite;
Every time I let him, the String would bust.
Your Donkey is better behaved, I trust.

The Hippo

A Head or Tail—which does he lack?
I think his Forward's coming back!
He lives on Carrots, Leeks and Hay;
He starts to yawn—it takes All Day—

Some time I think I'll live that way.

The Lamb

The Lamb just says, I AM!
He frisks and whisks, *He* can.
He jumps all over. Who
Are *you*? You're jumping too!

The Lizard

The Time to Tickle a Lizard,
Is Before, or Right After, a Blizzard.
Now the place to begin
Is just under his Chin,—
And here's more Advice:
Don't Poke more than Twice
At an Intimate Place like his Gizzard.

FROM THE NOTEBOOKS

"The desire to leave many poems in a state of
partial completeness;
to write nothing but fragments."
—from a note, ca. 1945

If you can't think, at least sing.

*

What dies before me is myself alone:
What lives again? Only a man of straw—
Yet straw can feed a fire to melt down stone.

*

To love objects is to love life.
The pure shaft of a single granary on the prairie,
The small pool of rain in the plank of a railway
      siding . . .

*

Dear God, I want it all: the depths and the heights.

*

You can't walk away from your own shadow;
I have observed the quiet around the opening flower,
The numinous ring surrounding the bud-sheathes . . .
The point is, dear father, if I don't stop soon,
I'm going to become a sun-tanned idiot boy . . .
I have basted the meat and eaten the bones;
I've kept grandpa from crying into his beard;
All I ask is a way out of slop;
Loose me into grace, papa,
I'm up to here and I can't stop.

I can't scratch anymore. My lips need more than a
    snifter.
Give me the pure mouth of a worm;
I'll feed on leaves; I'm a knob waiting for the opening
    squeak.
Why must I wait here, sitting on my hat?
Who else caught the burning bush?
I'm blistered from insights.
Several times I've heard the slow sigh of what is,
The moaning under the stones,
And the flames flashing off wings, burning but not
    consuming.
But then, what happened? I lapsed back into that same
    terrible calm,
No more than a nose in a grave, the pits of an ugly
    dream.

*

Deliver me from myself: my journeys are all the same,
    father.
Ends, ends, pursue me.

*

An intense terrifying man: eating himself up with rage.

*

Such a one as never milked a mother.

*

I practice at walking the void.

*

Why shouldn't I sing to myself?

*

And shall we leap the trees as light as birds?

*

I leap to the wind.

*

A stretching time, a crossing time,
Taller than the longest sun-shaft . . .

*

I cursed my being visible.

*

What eats us here? Is this infinity too close,
These mountains and these clouds? On clearing days
We act like something else; a race arrived
From caves . . .
Bearlike, come stumbling into the sun, avoid that shade
Still lingering in patches, spotting the green ground.

*

Summer stopped on the hill: the weeds came round;
Small breathers and sweaters, sly delicate algae . . .

*

Fish-mouths nudging against walls.
Moths hanging on harsh light.

*

Stared at the rock's vein, the light
In the round of my hand balanced a stone;
Among the ringed ponds, the warped sills, sun-blistered
        walls.

*

The true point of the spirit sways,
Not like a ghostly swan,
But as a vine, a tendril,
Groping toward a patch of light . . .

*

From this day count all time: I left him there,
Singing across that great abyss between us,
Goodbye . . .

*

In a deep deep yes. In all. I'm here alone and left.

*

The world is where we fling it.
Lift me, long dream.
I'm leaving where I am for other loves
Than what I see.

*

Time had no home in me.

*

Deep in their roots, all flowers keep the light.

*

What love-stirs! What loops and ropes of blossom!
Seed-skins kissed by the sun! The faint horns uncurling!
Bugs skimming through the oblique sunshafts!
And a song! Two songs, one outward, one inward
Echoing on each side of the glass,
One balanced on the edge of a wind-vent;
Another within, each singing things of the spirit,
This breathing, all upward, from leaves shining, wet,
The men wheeling in new dirt, their wheelbarrows
    creaking,
The sweat flashing on their faces, their palms wet,
Their palm-sweat flashing gold:
The day bright with its whiteness,
Those seeds in the next house already humping up dirt,
Heavy and hot. The bushels whisking past, that flip-flap
    familiar,—

I was more than child when I saw this,
And time was immediate.
Something more asks me now:
See deeper than this:
That was a bright dancing of shapes
Before the pits, the sour lakes of the self,
Those times when alone I spoke to the wall.
New motions began in me, there in the filth,
But I came back, still with my blood.
All myself, too happy to ask
Why I was not struck down: haunting the shade,
I held my heart.

*

How far's my father now?
Where has he gone, soft ears?
Tell me now. How far?
The sheep can't shear themselves.
Alone, alone, my cold ghost says.

*

Still air, still; almost noon.
The leaves dry on the trellis.
Will the green slime take fire, the slime on the benches?
This soil is past itself, half-gray, half-green . . .
The harp of the self stills.
Blue air, breathe on these nerves
Heat from the roses.
My hands are among blossoms,
Motion has narrowed,
My fingers natural.
Holding these, what do I hold?
More than a mold's kiss

Lifted into starlight,
Brought to this morning-shape.
My self breathes in these:
Star-flower, portal into the night,
Breathing brighter than water,
The twilight cannot whelm you.

*

Words for the wind, I know:
She, dreamily lascivious, like a seed,
Just new to sun and water, swelled within
Until her deepest being had to heed
The strict compulsion troubling all her skin.

*

Sweet stars, I'll ask a softer question: Moon
Attend me to the end. I'm here alone.

*

John Clare, I know the way your spirit went:
Day after day, the lonely languishment,
Hours turn to minutes when true spirits laugh:
He loved the world, and cut his life in half.

*

Christopher, help me love this loose thing.
I think of you now, kneeling in London muck,
Praying for grace to descend.

*

In that raw dark, in that black matted wood,
The final white, the mother-goddess stood.

*

For Father-Stem and Mother-Root—
The will sings to me now:
And all its notes are wild:

I'm quickened by a vow
To resurrect a child . . .

*

I remember more than the far sun
Touching the vine, or thc level light
Straight through the end panes . . .

*

From those lost depths, a childhood without love, some-
     thing may come anew, more real than it ever was.

*

I was born under a heavy shade,
Loam-fire my father.

*

The happy hats come at me.
I'm here but once.
I'm up, I'm up, you mother-melting flowers,
The dearest delver that ever was.

*

My face washed in the milk of this morning.

*

What wronged ghost raves in this house?
I cannot say. Time's dying on the moon.
I hear the minutes limping round and round.

*

He's here, the very father and son of death
Who shakes the dark with his look.

*

My long fathers are calling.
I hear the cries from the muck and sand . . .

*

Heart, you have no house.

*

I slept with Yes, but woke to No.

*

The exhausting fight against the inner fatigue, the soul-
    sickness.

*

The grandeurs of the crazy man alone,
Himself the middle of a roaring world.

*

To possess or be possessed by one's own identity?

*

The self, the anti-self in dire embrace.

*

The wing-tip of madness for Baudelaire: me, I live in
    the aviary.

*

In euphoria: a terrible fear that I would not live long
enough to achieve the full essence of experience.

*

I can't go on flying apart just for those who want the
benefit of a few verbal kicks. My God, do you know what
poems like that *cost*? They're not written vicariously:
they come out of actual suffering, *real* madness.

I've got to go beyond. That's all there is to it.

Beyond what?

The human, the human, you fool. Don't you see
what I've done. I've come this far, and now I can't stop.
It's too late, baby, it's too late.

*

Who else can tell me what I dare to say?
All things prepare for the mysterious day
We live yet do not live, perpetually.

*

The sense of something ripped out of a deep conscious-
  ness: Be still, great silence.

*

A man struggling to find his proper silence.

*

O my poor words, bear with me.

*

My name is numb.

*

I can project myself easier into a flower than a person.

*

I change into vegetables. First a squash, then a
turnip. Finally, embracing my sides, hugging myself in
the delights of self-possession, still a virgin to all rele-
vance, my leaves at once press and expand; I steam in the
morning mist.

I become a cabbage, ready for the cleaver, the close
knives.

I endure peculiar worms, green as my leaves, who
curl in the choice parts of my interior, my once so-
private world. But there is nothing I can do.

She deserts me for a blonder vegetable. Since then I
have been committed by my roots to a time and a place.

*

Getting loose: I took my place among the lashing eels.

*

And you, sweet dear, the mouse of joy,
Dance, dance, with the sad animals
And wear the shape the lions wear.

*

May I live on, in the bull's nose, in the drooping tail of a
sheep, in the sharp slide of the come-down hail, a hero to
ten stones, the calf's answer, smelling the halls with my
hairy heels.

*

The dark went out of my several selves at the coming of
    day;
I thanked God for giving me language back,
For a time at least; and my random rages are over.
I've written my whispers down: and spare the good
    sheets none;
Still, deeply still, a creature of serenity, a spider
    climbing a trellis,
I flew out upon the world.
And how I loved water, even a puddle shined with the
    face of the lord.

*

Greenhouse: this hell and heaven at once, this womb of
    cypress and double glass.

*

. . . And my father grew you in houses six hundred feet
    long, stems four and a half feet high
(Thirty-five dollars a dozen to select customers).
Once he lifted me up, only five,
To look at what he had created
With the liquid-manure machine and sixty-five men to
    help him,
To say nothing of God, THE FLORISTS' REVIEW,
    and the power of steam, sun and water,
They came out of a lovely tremendous stink, straight as
    bamboo in the stem,

Close-budded, wrapped in their secrets, vestal virgins,
How he hated to cut them!
And the men went in, secretly, in the early morning,
To gather their supply for the stores, and the funeral
    orders . . .
                        *
My grief was excessive, but I recovered.
For death-into-life was the rhythm of the greenhouse,
The men emptying the parched benches in the hot days
    of August,
Piling the gray exhausted earth outside,
Wheeling the shrunken stems, the maimed roots to the
    ever-changing flower-dump—
Then the seed, the seed, finer than rose-dust,
Renewing the new loam, finely sieved, under the sloped
    glass,
And the knobs of growth breaking from the tips of fresh
    cuttings,
In the flat boxes of sand, in the low side-benches,
The fuchsias, the swaying hydrangeas,
The callas, yellow at the tip, early in September,
The roses fading into wrinkled papery knobs.
                        *
The trees are gone, all the white glass is gone,
The concrete benches bolster paving-stone.

Once I was young, and walked a flowery way;
A greenhouse is its own eternity.
                        *
Form is a father: when I looked for form,
I found a leaf, and on the leaf a worm.

Whose lips dare speak? I fear the cold Therefore
And pass, unfeeling, at a feeling's grave:
A child died here. I was that likely child.

*

Now I must go beyond:
Who else knows where I am? I'm
A fish lurking close to a boat, a child holding the net,
I live through my black tears, a child of light.

*

Fleeing the heart's blankness, I turned to flowers . . .

*

All reality sleeps here, in the seed, in the stem . . .

*

The two duties are to lament or praise.

*

Between the soul and flesh
What war? I never heard:
I know a singing fish,
A silent bird.

*

The mire's my home! It always was my home.
Fair seed-time had my soul: foul was the edge
Beyond the undulant, the shimmering plain—
Less than the pensive bird, the single man
But half-himself, or something other than.

*

I know how flowers think. Behold in me
One who transcends the sensual ecstasy.
By grubbing among stones, in the close dirt,
I found out where my father left his heart . . .

*

Where my lost father is: there would I be.

*

Ceaseless the action of the water:
The little nudgings of the tide into the tiny rock-craters,
The waves like the skin of a fish,
Small, close, and all alike:
Then a sudden cross-riffle of wind changes all to a
     diagonal fluttering.

Then almost silence, almost a pond-shimmer.

A leaf falls on the sheep-path,
Loud as a step.
Another drops into the water,
Rides like a child's boat on the green debris, stiff as a
     shell,
Stiff as a broken nut-shell, floating
The undulant inch-long waves wrinkling toward
     me . . .

And time slows down, slows down.
The vine-like dead branches of the madrona arch over
     the water,
Creaking slightly with each light wind-shift;
The wave-shimmers play back on the parched leaves.

*

I would put myself, pit myself against oblivion.

*

My bones shrink to a bird;
I am less than a child,
A vein beating, unheard,
In the close, in the coming dark,
My spirit turns to its work.

*

My memory, my prison.

*

I am nothing but what I remember.

*

Greenhouse appeared in a dream as a sparkle of glass:
like dream of flat water: the calm, the eye of a pond.

*

What was the greenhouse? It was a jungle, and it was
paradise; it was order and disorder: Was it an escape?
No, for it was a reality harsher than reality.

*

I was never his son, not I.

*

I sank into the womb of the barn,
Grain scraping my soft underarms;
I lay under the benches, breathing with weeds,
Snails in my hair,
Weed-blistered, bloody-kneed,
Cursing my father's life,
Outcast who spit in the well,
Dropped like hay down the chute . . .

*

The intolerable sadness that comes when we are aware at
last of our own destiny.

*

To be weary of one's own individuality—is that to die?

*

For Lawrence and I are going the same way: down:
A loosening into the dark, a fine spume-drift,
The touch of waters: the dark whorls, the curled eddies.

*

My vision falling like a burning house.

*

All my lights go dark. I fold into black stone.

*

Make the language take really desperate jumps.

*

Remember: our deepest perceptions are a waste if we
have no sense of form.

*

Puts his thought in motion—the poet.

*

Rhythm depends on expecting.

*

A small thing well done is better than the pretentious
failure. If a thing fails rhythmically it's nothing.

*

Honesty: the only tricks of the real artist are technical.

*

I am a poet: I am always hungry.

*

There are so many ways of going to pot as a poet; so
many pitfalls, so many snares and delusions.

*

Live in a perpetual great astonishment.

*

Tennyson lay down with the words of the day.

*

Never be ashamed of the strange.

*

Those who are willing to be vulnerable move among
mysteries.

*

Get down where your obsessions are. For Christ's sake,
shake it loose. Make like a dream, but not a dreamy
poem. The past is asking. You can't go dibble dabble in
your tears. The fungi will come running; the mould will
begin all over the noble lineaments of the soul. Remember: a fake compassion covers up many a sore. Keep
more than your nose clean. Abstinence makes the heart
meander. Even the vapors are twitching. Certainly, flesh,
I hear you perfectly. But this time and place is for something else.
Sit here, the rocks are warm, sing the sirens,
Listen to them and your belly will soon be a pudding.
Instead, prance with the cats,
See what the soft woods say,
Let the nerves sing, and the soul, for the time being,
keep silent.
The eyes have it. Remember: the dead keep out the half-dead—
Those dreary language-arrangers. Don't be ashamed if
you belch when you try to sing. You may be a visceral
spinner . . .

*

Surround yourself with rising waters: the flood will teach
you to swim.

*

More than two days in Detroit is not permitted the human psyche.

*

It is well to keep in touch with chaos.

*

Exaggeration: a lovely thing but it must come naturally . . .

*

The body is the soul.

*

I trust all joy.

*

As if I'm being tortured by the gods—this feeling there is some great task just beyond, a new triumphant rhythm.

*

I am overwhelmed by the beautiful disorder of poetry, the eternal virginity of words.

BIOGRAPHICAL NOTE

NOTE ON THE TEXTS

NOTES

INDEX OF TITLES &
FIRST LINES

Theodore Roethke was born on May 25, 1908, in Saginaw, Michigan. His grandfather, who had been the chief forester on the estate of Bismarck's sister in Prussia, immigrated to the U.S. in 1872; his father ran the family's greenhouse business until it was sold in 1922, a year before he died of cancer. Roethke spent his childhood in Saginaw and entered the University of Michigan in 1925, going on to graduate summa cum laude. Following a brief enrollment at the university's law school, he transferred to the graduate school to pursue a master's degree in English. His first published poems appeared in the little magazine *The Harp* in June 1930, and soon he began placing poems in national publications such as *The New Republic* and *Sewanee Review*. In fall 1930 he entered the graduate school at Harvard and spent the academic year there before accepting a position as an instructor at Lafayette College in Easton, Pennsylvania, the first of several teaching appointments at colleges including Michigan State (1935), Pennsylvania State (1936–43, 1947), Bennington (1943–46), and the University of Washington (1947–1963). Roethke became renowned for his brilliance as a teacher and many of his students, such as the poets James Wright, Carolyn Kizer, and Richard Hugo, would acknowledge a debt to him. In November 1935, suffering the first of several mental breakdowns that would afflict him for the rest of his life, he was hospitalized for two months. The poems he wrote during the 1930s were collected in *Open House* (1941), his first book. In 1946 he won the first of two Guggenheim fellowships and spent most of the year in Saginaw, working on the poems in his next collection, *The Lost Son* (1948). Lauded by critics, this book was followed by *Praise to the End!* (1951) and *The Waking* (1953), a volume combining early and more recent work that was awarded the Pulitzer Prize. He married Beatrice O'Connell, who had been a student of his at Bennington. Roethke was the recipient of several fellowships and prizes, most notably the Bollingen Prize and the National Book Award for *Words for the Wind: The Collected Verse of Theodore Roethke* (1958), and a Fulbright award (1955–56) that enabled an extended stay in Italy. The second of two Ford Foundation grants allowed him to travel to Ireland and England in 1960–61. He also wrote children's verse, publishing *I Am! Says the Lamb* in 1961 and *Party at the Zoo* in 1963. On August 1, 1963, Roethke died of a heart attack while swimming in a friend's pool on Bainbridge Island, Washington. The manuscript he was preparing in his final days, *The Far Field*, was edited by his wife and published in 1964, and won the National Book Award. An inveterate notetaker, Roethke left behind a prodigious quantity of fragments of poems and prose; David Wagoner, one of Roethke's students, edited his notebooks and published a selection as *Straw for the Fire* in 1972.

NOTE ON THE TEXTS

In general, the poems in this volume are grouped according to their first publication in one of Theodore Roethke's books. The one exception to this arrangement is "Frau Bauman, Frau Schmidt, and Frau Schwartze," first published in book form in *The Waking* but appearing here as part of *The Lost Son*. In *The Waking* (and later in *Words for the Wind: The Collected Verse of Theodore Roethke*), Roethke included it with poems from *The Lost Son*; the present volume follows his placement of the poem in these two books.

With the exception of poems in *The Far Field* and the notebook fragments, the preferred sources of the poems are their final versions published during Roethke's lifetime. All but four of the poems in this volume that were first published in book form in *Open House* (1941), *The Lost Son and Other Poems* (1948), *Praise to the End!* (1951), and *The Waking* (1953) were collected in *Words for the Wind: The Collected Verse of Theodore Roethke* (Garden City, N.Y: Doubleday, 1958), and are printed here in the versions published in that book. "The Premonition" and "Highway: Michigan" are taken from *Open House* (New York: Knopf, 1941); the source for "Double Feature" and "River Incident" is *The Lost Son and Other Poems* (Garden City, N.Y: Doubleday, 1948).

Roethke was preparing *The Far Field* when he died in 1963. Supervised through the press by his wife, the collection appeared the following year, published by Doubleday; this edition is the source for the poems selected from *The Far Field* in the present volume.

All poems in the "Poems for Children" section are taken from *I Am! Says the Lamb* (Garden City, NY: Doubleday, 1961). The poet David Wagoner edited Roethke's notebooks in *Straw for the Fire: From the Notebooks of Theodore Roethke 1943–63* (Garden City, NY: Doubleday, 1972), which is the source of the notebook fragments printed here.

The texts of the original printings chosen for inclusion here are presented without change, except for the correction of typographical errors. Spelling, punctuation, and capitalization are often expressive features and are not altered, even when inconsistent or irregular. One error has been corrected: the line at 86.22 was inadvertently dropped in *The Far Field* and is restored here, following the text printed in *The Collected Poems of Theodore Roethke* (Garden City, NY: Doubleday, 1966).

NOTES

4.1–2   "Long . . . *Hopkins*]   From the closing of Gerard Manley Hop-
kins' poem "Inversnaid" (1881): "What would the world be, once bereft /
Of wet and of wildness? Let them be left, / O let them be left, wildness
and wet; / Long live the weeds and the wilderness yet."

64.1   Sir John Davies]   English poet (1560–1626).

94.26   Mnetha, mother of Har]   Character in Blake's cosmology; see
Blake's poem "Tiriel" (1789, pub. 1874).

127.1   *FROM THE NOTEBOOKS*]   The notebook fragments printed
here are taken from David Wagoner's edition, *Straw for the Fire: From the
Notebooks of Theodore Roethke 1943–63*. In editing this previously unpub-
lished material Wagoner arranged the fragments "dramatically, not nec-
essarily chronologically," as he wrote in the book's introduction. (It is
impossible to date precisely many of the fragments from Roethke's
many notebooks and unpublished writings.) His edition is divided into
groupings of "poetry" and "prose," although for some of the fragments
this distinction is ambiguous: many aphoristic single lines are catego-
rized as poetry, and lineated writings are sometimes grouped with the
prose. Wagoner arranged the fragments in sections with titles. The se-
lection in the present volume appears in *Straw for the Fire* under the fol-
lowing section headings:

POETRY

127.6–13   If you can't think . . . siding . . .]   From "Straw from the
Fire (1953–62)."

127.14–128.22   Dear God . . . void]   From "In the Lap of a Dream
(1948–49)."

128.23–129.3   Why shouldn't . . . sun-shaft . . .]   From "A Nest of
Light (1948–49)."

129.4–130.3   I cursed . . . Goodbye . . .]   From "The Loveless
Provinces (1948–49)."

130.4–8   In a deep . . . see]   From "All the Semblance, All the Loss
(1948–49)."

130.9–132.6   Time . . . whelm you]   From "The Stony Garden
(1949–50)."

132.7–13   Words . . . alone]   From "In the Bush of Her Bones
(1949–50)."

132.14–20   John . . . descend]   From "The Dark Angel (1950–53)."

132.21–22   In that . . . stood]   From "Love Has Me Haunted
(1950–53)."

132.23–133.14   For Father-Stem . . . morning]   From "Father-Stem
and Mother-Root (1951–53)."

133.15–22   What wronged . . . house.]   From "Heart, You Have No
House (1951–53)."

134.1–135.5   I slept . . . numb]   From "The Middle of a Roaring
World (1954–58)."

135.6–136.15   I can . . . lord]   From "I Sing Other Wonders
(1954–58)."

136.16–138.7   Greenhouse . . . light]   From "Recall This Heaven's
Light (1954–58)."

138.8–10   Fleeing . . . praise]   From "The Plain Speech of a Crow
(1954–62)."

138.11–14   Between . . . bird]   From "Between the Soul and the Flesh
(1957)."

138.15–19   The mire's . . . than]   From "The Mire's My Home
1959–63)."

138.20–139.1   I know . . . be]   From "My Flesh Learned to Die
(1959–63)."

139.2–21   Ceaseless . . . leaves]   From "And Time Slows Down
(1960–63)."

139.22   I would . . . oblivion]   From "The Thin Cries of the Spirit
(1959–63)."

140.1–5   My bones . . . work]   From "My Instant of Forever
(1959–63)."

140.5–141.6   My memory . . . stone]   From "All My Lights Go Dark (1943–47)."

141.7–18   Make the language . . . astonishment.]   From "The Poet's Business (1943–47)."

142.1–142.25   Tennyson . . . spinner]   From "Words for Young Writers (1948–49)."

142.26–143.2   Surround . . . psyche]   From "The Proverbs of Purgatory (1948–49)."

143.3–5   It is well . . . naturally . . .]   From "I Teach Out of Love (1949–53)."

143.6–7   The body . . . joy]   From "The Hammer's Knowledge (1954–58)."

143.8–9   As if . . . rhythm]   From "From Roethke to Goethe (1954–58)."

143.10–11   I am . . . words]   From "The Beautiful Disorder (1954–63)."

INDEX OF TITLES AND FIRST LINES

A deep dish. Lumps in it, 45
A gull rides on the ripples of a dream, 76
A Head or Tail—which does he lack?, 126
A kitten can, 41
A Lady came to a Bear by a Stream, 123
A river glides out of the grass. A river or a serpent, 30
A shell arched under my toes, 20
Against the stone breakwater, 113
All night and all day the wind roared in the trees, 2
At Woodlawn I heard the dead cry, 23

Bat, The, 3
Beast, The, 75
Big Wind, 11
By day the bat is cousin to the mouse, 3
By snails, by leaps of frog, I came here, spirit, 52

Came to lakes; came to dead water, 34
Cannas shiny as slag, 16
Carnations, 16
Child on Top of a Greenhouse, 15
Cow, The, 121
Cuttings, 7
Cuttings (later), 7

Dinky, 120
Dolor, 18
Donkey, The, 125
Double Feature, 19

Elegy, 107
Elegy for Jane, 63

Far Field, The, 97
Field of Light, A, 34
Flower Dump, 16
Forcing House, 8
Four for Sir John Davies, from*: 1. Dance*, 64
Frau Bauman, Frau Schmidt, and Frau Schwartze, 13
From the Notebooks, 127

Geranium, The, 111
Gone the three ancient ladies, 13

He was the youngest son of a strange brood, 108
Heard in a Violent Ward, 111
Her face like a rain-beaten stone on the day she rolled off, 107
Here from the field's edge we survey, 5
Heron, The, 3
Highway: Michigan, 5
Hippo, The, 126
How I loved one like you when I was little!—, 78

I came to a great door, 75
I circled on leather paws, 19
I Cry, Love! Love!, 55
I dream of journeys repeatedly, 97
I had a Donkey, that was all right, 125
I have known the inexorable sadness of pencils, 18
I Knew a Woman, 70
I knew a woman, lovely in her bones, 70
I miss the polished brass, the powerful black horses, 4
I Need, I Need, 45
I remember the neckcurls, limp and damp as tendrils, 63
I saw a young snake glide, 77
I strolled across, 21
I study the lives on a leaf: the little, 21

I wake to sleep, and take my waking slow, 65
If you can't think, at least sing, 127
I'll make it; but it may take me, 58
In a Dark Time, 116
In a dark time, the eye begins to see, 116
In a shoe box stuffed in an old nylon stocking, 110
In heaven, too, 111
In moving-slow he has no Peer, 122
In the long journey out of the self, 90
Is that dance slowing in the mind of man, 64
It's dark in this wood, soft mocker, 48

Journey to the Interior, 90

Kitty-Cat Bird, The, 124

Lady and the Bear, The, 123
Lamb, The, 126
Let others probe the mystery if they can, 118
Light Breather, A, 62
Lizard, The, 126
Long Alley, The, 30
"Long Live the Weeds," 4
Long live the weeds that overwhelm, 4
Long Waters, The, 94
Longing, The, 84
Love, love, a lily's my care, 66
Lost Son, The, 23

Meadow Mouse, The, 110
Meditation at Oyster River, 86
Meditations of an Old Woman, from: *First Meditation*, 79
Mid-Country Blow, 2
Minimal, The, 21
Moss-Gathering, 10
My Papa's Waltz, 17
My secrets cry aloud, 1

Night Crow, 20
Night Journey, 6
North American Sequence, 84
Nothing would sleep in that cellar, dank as a ditch, 8
Now as the train bears west, 6

O, Thou Opening, O, 58
O what's the weather in a Beard?, 120
Old Florist, 12
On love's worst ugly day, 79
On the Road to Woodlawn, 4
On things asleep, no balm, 84
Open House, 1
Orchids, 10
Otto, 108
Over the low, barnacled, elephant-colored rocks, 86

Pale blossoms, each balanced on a single jointed stem, 16
Pickle Belt, 17
Praise to the End!, 48
Premonition, The, 2
Pure Fury, The, 73

Return, The, 19
Right Thing, The, 118
River Incident, 20
Root Cellar, 8
Rose, The, 102

Sententious Man, The, 71
Sequel, The, 117
Serpent, The, 121
Shape of the Fire, The, 36
Sloth, The, 122
Slug, 78
Snake, 77
Spirit and nature beat in one breast-bone—, 71
Sticks-in-a-drowse droop over sugary loam, 7
Storm, The, 113
Stupor of knowledge lacking inwardness—, 73
Suddenly they came flying, like a long scarf of smoke, 115
Surly One, The, 74

That hump of a man bunching chrysanthemums, 12
The fruit rolled by all day, 17
The heron stands in water where the swamp, 3
The Kitty-Cat Bird, he sat on a Fence, 124
The Lamb just says, I AM!, 126

The spirit moves, 62
The Time to Tickle a Lizard, 126
The whiskey on your breath, 17
The wind billowing out the seat of my britches, 15
There are those to whom place is unimportant, 102
There Once was a Cow with a Double Udder, 121
There was a most Monstrous Whale, 125
There was a most odious Yak, 125
There was a Serpent who had to sing, 121
They lean over the path, 10
Thing, The, 115
This urge, wrestle, resurrection of dry sticks, 7
To loosen with all ten fingers held wide and limber, 10
Transplanting, 14

Under the concrete benches, 9
Unfold! Unfold!, 52

Vines tougher than wrists, 8

Waking, The, 21
Waking, The, 65
Walk in Late Summer, A, 76
Walking this field I remember, 2
Was I too glib about eternal things, 117
Watching hands transplanting, 14
Weed Puller, 9
Went weeping, little bones. But where?, 55
Whale, The, 125
What's this? A dish for fat lips, 36
When I put her out, once, by the garbage pail, 111
When I saw that clumsy crow, 20
When true love broke my heart in half, 74
Where Knock Is Open Wide, 41
Where were the greenhouses going, 11
Whether the bees have thoughts, we cannot say, 94
With Buck still tied to the log, on comes the light, 19
Words for the Wind, 66

Yak, The, 125